METRICS-BASED PROCESS MAPPING

Identifying and Eliminating Waste in Office and Service Processes

METRICS-BASED PROCESS MAPPING

Identifying and Eliminating Waste in Office and Service Processes

Karen Martin
Mike Osterling

CRC Press
Taylor & Francis Group
Boca Raton   London   New York

CRC Press is an imprint of the
Taylor & Francis Group, an **informa** business

CRC Press
Taylor & Francis Group
6000 Broken Sound Parkway NW, Suite 300
Boca Raton, FL 33487-2742

© 2013 by Taylor & Francis Group, LLC
CRC Press is an imprint of Taylor & Francis Group, an Informa business

No claim to original U.S. Government works

Printed in the United States of America on acid-free paper
Version Date: 2012912

International Standard Book Number: 978-1-4398-8668-7 (Paperback)

Library of Congress Cataloging-in-Publication Data

Martin, Karen.
   Metrics-based process mapping : identifying and eliminating waste in office and service processes / Karen Martin and Mike Osterling.
      p. cm.
   "Second edition of Metrics-Based Process Mapping"--Introduction.
   Includes bibliographical references and index.
   ISBN 978-1-4398-8668-7 (alk. paper)
   1. Industrial efficiency--Evaluation. 2. Industrial productivity--Measurement. 3. Production management. 4. Manufacturing processes. I. Osterling, Mike. II. Title.

T58.8.M37 2013
658.5'15--dc23
                                                                        2012034646

Visit the Taylor & Francis Web site at
http://www.taylorandfrancis.com

and the CRC Press Web site at
http://www.crcpress.com

Contents

Introduction

In the five years since we published *The Kaizen Event Planner*, in which we introduced Metrics-Based Process Mapping (MBPM), and the four years since we released the Excel tool to electronically capture one's results, Lean management practices have evolved. Where many of the early Lean books—and therefore field application—were heavily tools based, today's Lean practitioners, consultants, researchers, and business leaders recognize that, while tools are necessary, they are not sufficient. As we've explored more deeply what makes Toyota and other outstanding organizations tick, we've recognized that operational excellence and lasting transformation are the result of developing deep organizational capabilities around problem solving and continuous improvement.

We've also learned that proficiency in process measurement and analysis remains low, which slows improvement and creates significant risk when attempting to solve problems. Without a clear understanding of current-state performance, which requires the use of key process metrics, improvement teams risk drawing inappropriate conclusions and making improvement that is neither effective nor measurable. Let us be clear: it's impossible to make informed process design decisions and measure one's progress without relevant metrics.

For these two reasons, we've decided to release a second edition of *Metrics-Based Process Mapping*, which includes additional content based on current thinking in applying Lean practices, user feedback, and our observation that, while many businesses are making headway on their journey to excellence, nearly all could benefit by improving how they improve. We've also decided to convert it from a CD product that focuses more heavily on the Excel documentation tool to a book that focuses more heavily on the mapping methodology, but also includes the Excel documentation tool (on the CD attached to the back cover).

The new content includes:

- Foundational content about processes—what they are and how they vary
- A description of the difference between value-stream and process-level maps
- Additional content about how best to bridge the gap between the current state and your desired future state, and how to manage processes once improvement's been made
- A reminder that reducing mura (inconsistency) and muri (overburden)— initially overlooked in most Lean books—is as important as eliminating muda (waste)
- Tips for effective team formation and mapping facilitation
- On the Excel tool, we've added an implementation plan to aid those who are using the mapping methodology as a standalone tool and not part of a Kaizen Event

In Chapter 1, you'll learn what a process is, how processes vary, and why process management is critical to organizational excellence.

Chapter 2 focuses on why we developed this method, how to use it, its benefits, and how process mapping fits into the overall Plan-Do-Study-Adjust improvement cycle. Chapter 3 addresses preparation for mapping, including team formation, logistics, and crafting a charter that serves as a planning and communication tool.

The step-by-step approach for creating a current-state map is covered in Chapter 4. Here, we also introduce the three key metrics you need to gain a deep understanding of current state—process time, lead time, and percent complete and accurate—and design an improved process that reduces both time metrics, while increasing process quality.

Chapter 5 provides guidance for designing and implementing improvements to your process, while recognizing that every process's performance needs are different. To this end, we avoid prescription. We've also included some tips we use to counter resistance to improvement.

Chapter 6 serves as a user's guide for the Excel tool included on the CD in the back of this book, should you opt to electronically archive your mapping team's work and the new standard work for the improved process. And finally, Chapter 7 shows you how to monitor and continuously improve your processes, a step where organizations often falter.

As you begin reading, we encourage you to conduct an honest evaluation about where your organization currently sits in terms of process design, management, and improvement. We find that, even in organizations that have been applying Lean and/or Six Sigma practices for many years, processes remain largely undefined, riddled with waste, not monitored, and not continuously improved. The behaviors, habits, and practices that must be adopted in order to transform into an improvement-minded organization that performs at increasingly high levels are conspicuously absent in most companies, government agencies, and nonprofits. It's time to change that. It's time to put an end to organizational performance that limps along due to excess waste and confusion, the poor morale that results from poorly defined and managed processes, the leadership frustration and poor decisions that can result from not knowing how processes will perform tomorrow as compared to today, and customer experiences that make them more likely to turn elsewhere for solutions to their problems. It's time to put an end to the organizational chaos that holds you back from performing at the levels you want and need to. It's time to create a work environment that has fewer fires, happier employees, and the bandwidth to innovate and add customer value.

While this book provides the know-how for applying an effective tool for defining, improving, and managing processes, it does not include detailed content about how to create a culture where metrics-based process mapping is used as the means to build the organization discipline needed for continuous improvement. Ideally, nearly everyone in your organization knows how to create MBPMs and they are highly proficient in thinking about processes in terms of the three key metrics: process time, lead time, and percent complete and accurate.

Your ultimate goal is to operate with processes that are well-defined, error-proofed, standardized as much as is prudent, waste-free, documented, and regularly monitored. We've written this book and developed an Excel tool that has proven to be helpful to many. We hope you find this to be the case as well and welcome you to share your experiences by contacting Karen at www.ksmartin.com and Mike at www.mosterling.com.

Now, let's get to it. There's much to be done.

Chapter 1

What Is a Process?

How many times have you heard, said, or felt, "Well, that was a grueling process"? Whether you are grocery shopping, filing an insurance claim, or trying to get through the security line at the airport, we are surrounded by processes. Some go so smoothly we hardly take note; others can be downright painful.

In the work environment, processes are how all needs or requests are satisfied. More and more organizations are beginning to understand that they need to improve their processes. In fact, they need to be *continuously* improved. But before we can discuss how to improve processes, it is helpful to understand what a process is, what the common components are, the types of processes, and why process management is important.

Definition of a Process

Merriam-Webster defines a process as "a series of actions or operations conducing to an end." Taking this definition to the next level, a process is a sequence of activities performed to design, produce, or deliver a good or service to an internal or external customer. In the Lean vernacular, processes are classified as either *value-adding* or *non-value-adding* as viewed through the eyes of an external customer. Non-value-adding processes are further classified as either necessary (essential for meeting business requirements) or unnecessary (nonessential). Necessary non-value-adding processes are sometimes referred to as *value-enabling* processes.

The individual steps one takes to get work done (or the specific tasks one performs) connect together to form processes, and processes connect together to create value streams, the way in which you deliver value to your customers. We discuss value streams in greater detail in Chapter 2.

Process Components

A process has three primary components: inputs, activities, and outputs. Process *inputs* may be verbal (phone calls and in-person requests), electronic (orders, reports, downloads, e-mail requests, etc.), physical (e.g., hard copy reports and forms, service parts, equipment, specimens for analysis, etc.), or human (people seeking a service). Process *outputs* are typically the product (good, service, or information) required by the customer of the process.

Process *activities* are the actions that are taken to convert inputs into outputs. Many of these activities could be classified as transformational (e.g., calculating a price in response to a request for a quote); other activities do not transform inputs but are still classified as work (e.g., moving a document from one person to another, etc.).

Documenting process inputs, activities, and outputs serves a variety of purposes. First, formally and clearly defining customer requirements and expectations is necessary to ensure that process outputs are properly designed and delivered. The quality of process outputs is directly related to the quality and consistency of process inputs and the process design itself. Second, understanding and documenting inputs and activities is necessary to identify and eliminate wasteful activities that add expense, slow delivery, erode quality, create unnecessary risk, and frustrate employees, customers, and other stakeholders. Finally, process documentation is also necessary for training process workers, measuring process performance, and serving as the foundation of continuous improvement.

Types of Processes

In considering process improvement, it is helpful to understand the different types of processes. Some processes involve a physical transformation such as repairing a computer or baking a cake. Other processes convey information such as a loan approval. And other processes transform information into knowledge such as the design of a new product or service.

Processes range from low to high variation. In a low-variation process, the inputs, activities, and outputs are fairly consistent—for example, processing loan payments or insurance claims. In higher-variation processes, the inputs, activities, and outputs may vary significantly, both in terms of the type of input, activity or output, and the time it takes to accomplish the work. Processes ultimately serve either internal or external customers, and receive initial inputs from either internal or external suppliers. For example, expense report processing serves an internal customer (the employee), whereas processing a credit application serves an external customer (the applicant). And, in some cases, the suppliers are both internal and external, as is found in an estimating process that requires cost inputs from both manufacturing and external subcontractors. And, in many office and service processes, the customer and the supplier may be one and the same, as is found in credit application and expense report processes.

Other ways in which processes can be differentiated include the frequency with which the process is performed (repetitive or one time), technology used (automated versus manual), and the mental processes involved (analytical versus rote).

Process Management

Processes that are properly defined, and executed will produce predictable results, and in today's work environment, demands for well-executed processes are coming from all directions. External customers demand predictability in delivery and quality. To stay competitive, owners and managers constantly seek cost reductions, better quality, and faster delivery. The workforce wants greater engagement, reduced interpersonal and interdepartmental friction, and less frustration and stress while performing their jobs. Poor process management can hinder the realization of all of these needs. By understanding process inputs and focusing on improving how the work is done, outputs can be measurably improved. But improvement can only be achieved if you know how the process is performed, you can measure process performance, and you have the ability to see where the gaps exist within the process. This is where Metrics-Based Process Mapping comes into the picture.

Chapter 2

What Is Metrics-Based Process Mapping (MBPM)?

Effective process improvement is similar to a well-planned trip. You need to know more than simply the starting point and destination for the journey. You also need to know the specific route you will take to get there. But if you are not clear about the current state, you may select a path that leads you off course, slowing or blocking your ability to reach your destination.

Establishing a clear understanding of the current state is also vital because, while individuals are experts in the process steps they perform on a daily basis, typically no one on a mapping team—in fact, no one in the entire organization—understands the complete process for producing and delivering the organization's good(s) or service(s). It is difficult to design an improved state if a team charged with making improvement does not fully understand the current state, including the true customer requirements, the quality of existing inputs and outputs, and the downstream impact of design decisions they may make regarding upstream process steps.

Metrics-Based Process Mapping (MBPM) is a methodology that enables improvement teams to perform the type of detailed current-state analyses that are often required to design process-level improvements. In organizations that use value stream mapping (VSM) as a strategic improvement planning process and macro-level performance assessment tool (Figure 2.1), MBPM is used as a next step to understand current performance at a more granular level and to design tactical-level improvements. For organizations that use A3 management to problem solve, make improvements,

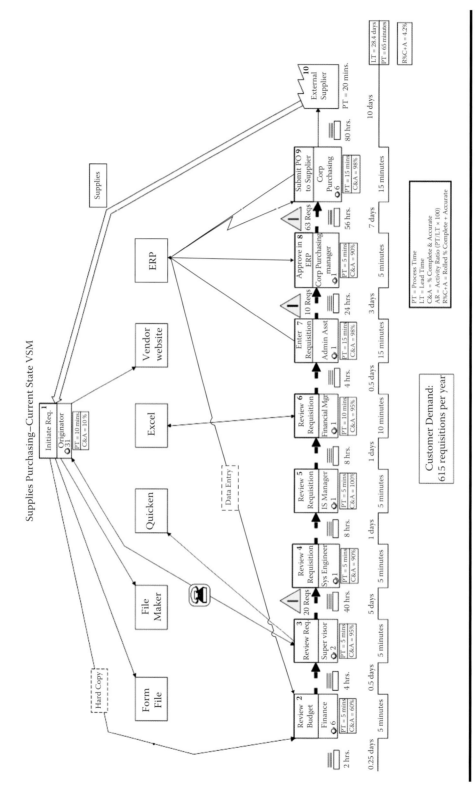

Figure 2.1   Current-state value stream map: purchasing process.

and manage development projects, MBPM is an effective tool for grasping the current condition at a granular level. For organizations unfamiliar with value stream mapping or A3 management, MBPM is an effective standalone tool for analyzing and designing new processes using more traditional operations improvement methods. In all cases, MBPM enables improvement teams to get into the weeds and "peel back the layers of the onion" to see the "waste behind the waste." For example, a value stream map may reveal excessively long lead times or poor quality output for a particular process. The MBPM can reveal the specific reasons for the long lead times or poor quality output that the value stream map revealed. The future-state VSM and the accompanying implementation plan serve as your strategic plan. A process-level map enables deeper analysis in a more narrowly defined portion of the value stream and defines executable, tactical improvements.

We developed the Metrics-Based Process Mapping (MBPM) technique to fill a void that existed in the process analysis world. None of the traditional process mapping techniques provided both the ability to analyze processes from a functional perspective *and* use metrics to drive future-state design decisions. And, where manufacturing had long relied on line-balance charts and standard work combination sheets to analyze production-related process steps, an equivalent analytical tool didn't exist for office, service, and knowledge-work processes. Thus, the MBPM was born, which integrates the strongest elements of two existing analytical tools: (1) the functional orientation of traditional swim-lane process maps, which helps us visualize cross-functional relationships and handoffs, and (2) the time and quality metrics that were introduced with the advent of value stream mapping, which help us quantify process performance and make it easier to see waste.

As you'll notice in Figure 2.2, the MBPM is not a process flow diagram. While process flow diagrams are valuable training tools, they lack metrics, and therefore are not effective tools for quantifying disconnects, bottlenecks, poor quality, and delays. Without metrics, teams may focus on irrelevant solutions that don't ultimately impact the two keys to efficient and effective process performance—quality and speed. And if you haven't established a baseline for how a process is performing, how can you measure your improvements? In today's return-on-investment environment—and in the interest of selling an improvement team's results—improved processes can't just *feel* better. They need to be *measurably* better, and improvement teams can't assess if processes truly are better unless they have an effective tool by which to measure them.

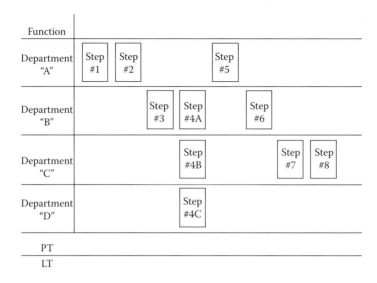

Figure 2.2   MBPM elements: Swim lanes house functions; Post-its® depict the sequential steps in the process, and a timeline shows the progression of work.

Organizations often confuse VSM with process-level mapping. Here are a few differentiators as we see them:

■ VSMs typically represent a *closed loop* from customer request to delivery, whereas the MBPM can be used to depict any part of a process or VSM segment.
■ Current-state VSMs depict macro views of how work gets done; current-state MBPMs depict micro views, similar to zooming in on a geographic map to see the names of individual streets.
■ Future-state VSMs serve as strategic planning tools that depict *what* has to happen to realize the future state; future-state MBPMs are tactical execution tools that show specifically *how* work will be done.
■ VSMs are visual storyboards that have three distinct components: material flow, information flow, and a timeline that reveals obstacles to work flow. The MBPM also has a timeline, but on an MBPM, material and information flow are merged together to provide very specific details on how information is entered and accessed.
■ The "blocks" on a VSM typically represent chunks of work—sometimes entire processes that link together to create a value stream. Some sort of delay typically exists between process blocks, such as the accumulation of work in process (WIP) because the receiving work area doesn't

have the capacity to begin work right away, or work sitting because no one knows it has arrived. The blocks on an MBPM represent specific tasks or steps in a process. Therefore, one VSM block might result in 2, 10, or even 20 blocks on an MBPM. Similarly, VSM blocks typically represent handoffs to new work areas, whereas you might have several sequential blocks on an MBPM that represent a single person's work.

Putting this all together, here's how you might use the two types of maps together. Let's say you have a process where the lead times are too long. Creating a VSM will reveal delays in the timeline that contribute to the long lead times, but not necessarily the specific reasons for the extended lead times, such as rework loops, multiple handoffs, excessive review, redundant data entry, interruptions, multitasking, and so on. An improvement team charged with reducing the lead time will need to understand *why* the waste exists—the fundamental *root causes* or underlying problems that produces the symptoms of waste that the VSM reveals—before they can determine the appropriate *countermeasure*[*] they'll use to shorten the lead time. So, at a macro level, you may know you need to shorten the lead time, but you need micro-level data to determine how to best accomplish that objective.

How do you decide if you'll need an MBPM? The VSM typically determines whether you need to drill down to the micro level and get into the details. You will find the MBPM to be a useful tool when the VSM reveals opportunities for improvement, but it is not clear what specific issues are contributing to prolonged lead times, excessive process times, or poor quality.

If, on the other hand, your VSM depicts a process riddled with handoffs that are merely reviews and approvals, you won't gain significantly more information about the waste by creating an MBPM. In this case, the solution for shortening lead time to the customer and improving quality is obvious: reduce the number of approvals. Implementing this improvement requires the creation of standard work and some cross-training for the people performing the remaining approval steps, but an MBPM is not needed to make these determinations.

You should use the MBPM method when your improvements require a fair amount of investigation and analysis to determine the true underlying cause(s) for the process performance issues that the value stream map has revealed.

---

[*] We prefer the term countermeasure over solution and discuss this further in Chapter 5.

We're asked the opposite question a fair amount as well—when should you move directly to a process-level map and forego value stream mapping? In our opinion, not very often. Value stream mapping not only helps put processes into proper context and trains people to think holistically, but it also serves as an effective consensus-building tool, which can reduce the resistance to change when you begin discussing the nitty-gritty details of how people perform their work. Once people understand the big picture and see the problems from a macro level, it's more difficult for them to say, "Nah, we don't want to change." After seeing very obviously the need for improvement at a macro level, improving at the micro level grows easier.

Another reason you don't want to forego value stream mapping, except for very rare circumstances, is psychological. First, the mind can only grasp so much complication at once. You'll get further faster if you take improvement in phases and begin with a less complicated (macro) view of how work gets accomplished, and then make your way into the significant complication that often exists at a process level (especially for processes that haven't been through an initial round of improvement). Second, beginning at the value stream level helps people see the similarities in how what they perceive to be high-variation work flows through the system versus the initial belief we hear commonly: "Everything we do is different; therefore, it cannot possibly be standardized." Looking at work from a holistic perspective helps illustrate how the people, their work, and their work systems are more similar than previously believed. This shift in thinking is beneficial as you begin designing the future state.

The two biggest mapping problems we continue to see are: (1) people are still confusing value stream and process-level mapping, and (2) outside of manufacturing, both types of maps often lack metrics, one of the nonnegotiable aspects of value stream and process level maps. Figure 2.3 depicts the difference between value stream and process-level maps.

Value stream maps are not structured as swim lane-style maps. Rather, they are storyboards that visually depict the full cycle of delivering value to a customer (whether external or internal) from the customer's initial request or order to receiving the good or service requested. The blocks in a value stream map represent major activities between which the work in question sits idle for any number of reasons. In a metrics-based process map, you delineate the individual steps required to complete those major activities.

Another key feature and benefit of the value stream map is that the flow of information is visually depicted so we can see at a macro level how work

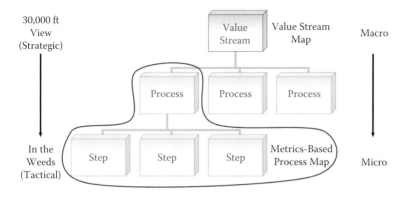

Figure 2.3   The difference between value stream and process maps.

is scheduled (if it's scheduled at all), who tells whom to do what, and which IT systems and applications are involved. The metrics-based process map does not capture these visual details as it is not a macro-level storyboard. If you skip value stream mapping, you lose the ability for all in the organization to see the disconnects, barriers to flow, and complication in your current IT and human communication systems.

Before we dive into mapping itself, there are two more key issues you need to consider: (1) the way in which you strategically go about selecting processes to be improved, and (2) the method you'll use to move most effectively from intention to results.

Strategic and Methodological Improvement

As we mentioned in the introduction, the Lean community's collective understanding about Lean business practices has grown significantly. Researchers such as Jeffrey Liker (*The Toyota Way*) and Mike Rother (*Toyota Kata, Learning to See*) have provided us with deep and ongoing new insights into how and why Toyota operates the way it does. This growing knowledge base has helped all of us see that our initial fascination with tools, while understandable, was short-sighted.

Was it wrong to focus on building proficiency in creating value stream maps, implementing effective Kanban systems, and 5Sing every nook and cranny around? No. You'd have to build proficiency at some point. But we've reached a crossroads where unless we incorporate a more deliberate approach to improvement and move away from the "random acts of

Kaizen" that often characterized the first decade of the Lean movement, we risk never achieving the bottom line impact that Lean can so richly deliver.

How do we become more deliberate? By creating annual improvement plans that align with an organization's business goals, tying all we do to solving carefully defined problems, and employing the scientific method to making improvement via PDSA: Plan-Do-Study-Adjust.*

It's beyond the scope of this book to address creating an improvement strategy and there are many good resources to turn to for that. It's also beyond the scope of this book to delve into the various methods in which you can develop deep problem-solving and improvement capabilities by using PDSA. But we will explain how metrics-based process mapping fits into the PDSA cycle.

The "P" in PDSA—Plan—includes gaining a deep understanding about the current state, establishing a target condition, and identifying both the root causes for the current process performance and the obstacles to achieving the target condition. To date, we have found no more effective method than MBPM for defining and analyzing the current state of office and service processes at a detailed level.

On the other end of the cycle, the "A" stage—Adjust—requires us to continuously monitor the key performance indicators we've established, and begin new PDSA cycles both when corrective action is warranted and to make additional improvement (establish a new target condition) to raise the performance bar higher and higher. Here, too, MBPM is a helpful ally. Once your future state becomes your current state, the MBPM can be used to continuously monitor process performance and determine where performance is beginning to erode. The MBPM serves as your map to make sure you stay on course—until the point where you decide to travel to a new destination, which requires you to create another map.

Finally, the MBPM should be used to train all new hires and transfers into the areas that touch the process. It's critical that all parties understand their role in the process, what the expectations are for the quality of the inputs they receive and the outputs they deliver, the timeframe for doing so, and the work effort they should expend doing the work. We recommend physically posting the MBPM in the areas that touch

---

* We're using PDSA instead of PDCA (plan-do-check-act) because we've come to understand that W. Edwards Deming felt that PDSA most closely aligned with Walter Shewart's original intent for the improvement cycle. In addition, we find (as did Deming) that people often misconstrue what is meant by "check" and "act." The terms "study" and "adjust" are more precise, linguistically.

the process and allow the people who do the work to use it as a living document, marking it up with additional improvement ideas to reduce waste further.

Now it's time to learn how to create an MBPM. We begin where we always begin: Planning—the "P" in Plan-Do-Study-Adjust.

Chapter 3

Mapping Preparation

Many of you will create MBPMs during Kaizen (rapid improvement) events, where the scope has already been defined and a team is already formed.* This chapter provides planning and logistics guidance for those who are using MBPM as a standalone tool outside of Kaizen events.

We recommend the use of charters to plan, communicate, and build consensus around all improvement activities. The Excel tool on the CD in the back of this book includes such a charter (sixth tab), shown in Figure 3.1.

While we aren't going to go into detail about every section of the charter, we will offer some pointers and considerations we find many planning teams overlook that will determine the degree of success you'll experience with your mapping endeavors.

But before we get into the specific charter elements, let's talk about who creates the charter. We recommend you involve three key people:

1. **Executive sponsor:** We find that improvement efforts that are overseen by an executive sponsor generally get better results and have a higher chance of being sustained than those where middle managers are leading the effort—especially for processes that are highly cross-functional in nature. This assumes, of course, that the sponsoring executive is an active sponsor versus an "in name only" sponsor. Depending on the maturity and experience of your leadership team, you may need to provide some gentle coaching to assure that executive sponsors are effective in their role.

---

* For more information about planning and executing Kaizen events, please refer to our first book, *The Kaizen Event Planner: Achieving Rapid Improvement in Office, Service, and Technical Environments.* (CRC Press, 2007).

Metrics-Based Process Mapping Charter

Improvement Scope		Leadership		Mapping Schedule	
Value Stream		Executive Sponsor		Date(s)	
Process Name					
Specific Conditions		Value Stream Champion		Start/End Times	
Customer Demand		Facilitator		Location	
Trigger					
First Step		Team Lead		Meals Provided	
Last Step					
Boundaries & Limitations		Briefing Attendees		Briefing Dates/Times	
FS Implementation Timeframe				Logistics Coordinator	

Improvement Drivers / Current State Issues		Mapping Team		
1			Function	Name
2		1		
3		2		
4		3		
5		4		
Improvement Goals & Measurable Objectives		5		
1		6		
2		7		
3		8		
4		9		
5		10		

Potential Deliverables		On-Call Support		
1			Function	Name	Contact Information
2		1		
3		2		
4		3		
5		4		

Possible Obstacles		Approvals		
1		Executive Sponsor	Facilitator	Team Lead
2				
3		Signature:	Signature:	Signature:
4		Date:	Date:	Date:

Figure 3.1 Metrics-Based Process Mapping Charter.

2. **Facilitator:** All mapping activities need to be led by an impartial and skilled facilitator, whether internal or external to your organization. With rare exceptions, mapping activities that are led by people who are directly involved in the process being improved are generally not able to maintain the level of objectivity that's needed to properly facilitate team-based activities.[*]

3. **Value Stream Champion:** The value stream champion is a person, typically at a manager or director level, who's responsible for the largest part of the process being improved. In highly siloed organizations where true value stream champions don't exist, this person is often the manager or director of the functional area that comprises the largest number of steps in the process. The value stream champion doesn't typically serve on the mapping team directly. Rather, he/she is the person the facilitator and team consult regarding obstacles to success, policy questions, and so on.

---

[*] You may wish to refer to *The Kaizen Event Planner* for additional information about the necessary skills and traits for effective facilitation.

4. **Team Lead:** A team lead is often helpful in coordinating mapping logistics and serving as the facilitator's go-to person during the mapping activity. Not all mapping activities require a team lead but, if one exists, this person should be engaged in all aspects of planning, including charter formation.

Now that we know who creates the charter, let's look at a few of the key elements of scoping and team formation.

Scoping the Process Being Mapped

To prepare for mapping, scope the process for analysis by first defining the specific conditions to be analyzed. To effectively analyze a process, your scope should be narrow and deep. For example, instead of mapping the order entry process for all products, all clients, all locations, and all seasons, you may need to focus on a specific condition, such as international orders for ABC product. Or instead of mapping the individual steps for an entire range of healthcare services, you may need to focus on one type of diagnostic procedure. This *narrowing* activity enables a more detailed and focused study and avoids designing a general solution that doesn't adequately address the specific issue at hand. Naturally, the improvement should fit as broad a set of circumstances as possible. The specific conditions for analysis are highly dependent on the problem you're attempting to solve. So if you lack clarity about the problem, your scoping may be off.

Once the specific conditions have been selected, define the beginning and ending "fence posts"—the first and last steps—within which the team will focus their efforts. Once you've clarified the problem you wish to solve and have scoped the activity, then and only then are you in a position to form the mapping team. Many organizations reverse these two steps and form the team prematurely. Team composition is 100 percent dependent on the process steps and the specific work conditions upon which the mapping activity will focus.

Forming the Mapping Team

When used within a Kaizen Event, the mapping team is the Kaizen Team. When used outside a Kaizen Event, the team should include at least one representative from each of the functional areas that are involved in the process. By *involved*, we mean upstream suppliers of information or material, the process workers themselves, and downstream customers, whether internal or external, who receive the output from the process steps being reviewed.

The mapping team should consist of no more than 10 people and be heavily biased (75 percent or so) toward those who do the work being improved on a daily basis and not solely those who supervise such activities. A member who serves as "outside eyes" with no "skin in the game" can be highly beneficial, though an impartial facilitator can also serve in this role. We also find that, since most office processes are IT-dependent, it's highly beneficial to have a full-time IT representative on the team.

One cautionary note: Team formation should be highly strategic and, therefore, will likely take many conversations with many people before the team is set. Another note: It's risky to rely on someone to provide the perspective for a function he or she used to represent. Work content knowledge becomes out of date nearly the moment someone leaves a role. Processes and the conditions under which they operate change frequently so relying on historical information, no matter how recent, is likely not reliable.

A final note: In case you're tempted to vary the team composition for creating the current- and future-state maps, don't. The same team that documents the current state should design the future state, to assure that those determining the countermeasures they'll use to bridge the gap between current and desired process performance fully understand the current-state details that are driving the need for improvement. The countermeasures begin revealing themselves as the current-state MBPM is being created, so if the people designing the future state have not been part of the current-state MBPM mapping team, they miss out on a significant benefit of being a part of current-state documentation, slowing the future-state design process. Given the detailed nature of an MBPM, significant rework can be required to get a team member up to speed.

Mapping Logistics

Depending on process complexity, you will need one to two days to create the current-state and future-state MBPMs, prioritize opportunities for improvements, and create an executable work plan.

In addition, since MBPMs contain micro-level process details and most processes are in constant flux to accommodate shifting business needs, creating the future-state MBPM should immediately follow—ideally on consecutive days—the creation of the current-state MBPM. Doing so avoids the mental setup required and rework that occurs when time has passed between current-state documentation and improvement design.

We recommend you hold the mapping activity on-site so the team can contact others who they may need to discuss ideas with, get metrics from, and so on. For the best results, the mapping activity needs to be conducted in a room with adequate wall space and enough room for the cross-functional team to gather around the map. If possible, remove art and other wall hangings to provide a flat surface. You'll also need enough room to accommodate a larger team that will be present for briefings on one or two of the days.

In terms of supplies, you'll need the following:

- 36-inch-wide white plotter paper[*]
- Scissors
- Masking tape
- Yard stick, chalk line, or other straight edge (for drawing functional swim lanes)
- 4 × 6 inch and smaller Post-its® in various colors
- Sharpies (or other medium-point markers)
- Calculators
- 1 or 2 flip charts and easels

When possible, we recommend that you create a central place for storing key mapping supplies, whether a designated closet, a rolling container, or a portable carryall.

Communication and Data Gathering

Once the charter is complete and all team members have been notified, the charter should be distributed to all relevant leadership and work teams

---

[*] If you're going to do a lot of mapping and you don't have an in-house large format (plotter) printer that uses 36-inch-wide paper, we recommend you purchase a large roll from a local printer. You can also buy rolls through office supply stores, but they're more expensive. Visit http://www.mbpmapping.com to download a template for eight-foot segments of 36-inch paper with prelined swim lanes.

and physically posted in all affected work areas. At this point, it's helpful to begin soliciting input from all parties involved—especially those who aren't on the team. Placing a whiteboard or flip chart in the affected work areas is a great way to collect information about the current state, build consensus about the type of improvements that will be needed, provide a feeling of inclusion for those who aren't part of the mapping team, and gather improvement ideas for the team's consideration.

At this point, the facilitator, team lead, or value stream champion (or a combination thereof) should be gathering relevant data about the process being improved: work volumes, output frequency, queue volumes, input and output quality, throughput time, process performance, customer expectations, process variation, and so on.

Once all of these tasks are complete, you're ready to move into the "D" stage—Do—of the Plan-Do-Study-Adjust (PDSA) cycle and begin creating the current-state MBPM.

Chapter 4

Mapping Essentials: Understanding the Current State

This chapter represents the single most important step in the improvement process, and unfortunately the one that's often not well executed. While gaining clarity around the problem you wish to address is a critical first step, it's only part of the clarity you need to achieve the levels of performance you need and want. The second part of the clarity equation is gaining a deep understanding of how a process currently performs.

Many well-intentioned managers and improvement teams attempt to skip this vital step. We often hear, "But we don't have a current process in place to even map," to which we say, "Yes, you do." If you're performing work, you have a process. You may have many different processes to perform work—and each of them may suffer from high degrees of variation—but you do have defined processes, no matter how effective they are. The other counter we hear is, "It's so messed up that we want to start from a clean slate," again thinking that mapping the current state is a wasted effort.

Make no mistake about it: If you don't do the heavy lifting to understand all of the ins and outs of how you currently perform, no matter how difficult it is to gain this level of clarity, you'll miss the key learning that you need to design an effective future state. In addition, gaining a deep understanding of how you currently operate, no matter how ugly it may be, creates the proper mental framework—the psychological readiness—to embrace change. If the people involved don't see the reason why an improvement is being suggested, which they learn through mapping the current state, you're far more likely to experience resistance to the improvements being suggested. And, regardless of the level of resistance, it's far more difficult to experience *sustainable* improvement if people don't first see the unvarnished truth about how the process is currently performing.

Before we get into the specific how-tos for creating the current-state map, there are a few more preparation steps that are needed—hanging the paper. Prior to the team arriving, take the following steps:

1. Estimate the length of 36-inch-wide paper you will need and add 50 percent more. Cut it accordingly and affix it to the wall with masking tape (or push pins, if allowed). Mapping tip: Consider the mapping facilitator's and team members' heights when hanging the paper.
2. Draw 6 horizontal swim lanes across the paper, each 6 inches tall.[*] For complex processes with more than 6 functional areas involved, you may need to hang 2 rows of the mapping paper.
3. Draw a vertical line 4 to 6 inches from the left edge of the paper to house the swim lane labels for each functional area involved.

Once the room is set and the team has arrived, we recommend an official kickoff of some sort. At the very least, the executive sponsor or value stream champion (or equivalent) should greet the team, express his or her gratitude for the team's time, clarify expectations, and communicate his or her faith in the team and the facilitator. You may also want to include a brief overview about process design in general, the process for making and sustaining improvement, Lean philosophy and practices, and so on. If the team members have never worked together, you may also wish to include an ice breaker. We also recommend asking the team to agree to defined "rules of engagement"[†] that accelerate progress and set the stage for successful outcomes. The facilitator should also review the charter in detail to remind the team about the reasons why improvement is necessary, the process fence posts (first and last steps), and the specific conditions they're going to focus on.

Finally, the facilitator should let the team know that they are not allowed to consult written procedures, manuals, and process flow charts until *after* they have created the current-state MBPM and then, only to

---

[*] You can hand draw the lines, use a chalk line marking device (available at hardware stores), or download the preprinted PDF template we mentioned in Chapter 3 at www.mbpmapping.com.
[†] See *The Kaizen Event Planner* (CRC Press, 2007) for a detailed list of the rules of engagement we've found to be most helpful for team-based improvement activities.

assure that the team members did not overlook relevant process steps. Otherwise, they may be tempted to use these written "standardized" documents to depict the current state as it should be rather than how it actually *is*—how people actually do the work today.

With these preliminary steps completed, the team is now ready to begin mapping. There are two final preparation steps that begin the process of mapping:

1. On the left side of the map, list the functional departments that "touch" the process between and including the fence posts—the starting and ending steps within which the process will be mapped. These functional labels define the swim lanes within which the team will map each functional area's role in the process. If work product (paper, information, or material) is being passed from person to person within a department, you should dedicate a swim lane for each individual. The objective is to identify all handoffs.
2. In the upper right corner, write the map's title (e.g., Current-State MBPM); the process name; date; customer demand (volume of work per week, month, or year); and the team members' names.

The current-state MBPM is created in three phases—or passes. In other words, the team looks at the process three times to get the deep level of understanding you need to design an effective future state. During the first pass, the team defines how the process currently operates—who passes work and/or information to whom and in what sequence. Here, the team tracks how information, material, and/or people flow through the process, including the various system tools and applications involved, identifying process inputs and outputs along the way. (*Note:* It is also possible that the subject of the process is stationary and the process steps occur *around* the stationary subject, rather than the subject being passed through a process.) During the second pass, the team adds key metrics for each process step, including process time (PT), lead time (LT), and percent complete and accurate (%C&A), creates the timeline, and calculates key summary metrics. During the third pass, the team differentiates value-adding activities from non-value-adding work.

In some cases the team creates the map itself with the facilitator serving as a guide, and in others, the facilitator demonstrates the mapping process by completing the steps as the team provides input. We've found a combination to be the most effective means for meeting the concurrent needs of developing mapping capabilities across the organization and generating results. The remainder of this chapter lists the step-by-step process for creating the current-state map.

First Pass: Identify the Process Steps

The facilitator or the team members themselves documents each process step on a 4 × 6 inch Post-it®. Different colors may be used to depict the various functional departments, if desired, or to depict different individuals within a functional swim lane who perform the identified tasks. A process step is defined as a single activity or series of minor activities that are typically performed in a continuous time period, producing an output that is passed to another individual, team, or department for the next task to occur. A separate process step (requiring a separate Post-it) exists if:

■ A physical handoff occurs (work is passed from one person to another)
■ A delay exists within the process step
■ Multiple IT systems are accessed
■ A batch is created
■ Separate quality issues are identified for specific process step components

As shown in Figure 4.1, the process steps are documented by briefly describing the activity in the upper portion of the Post-it, using a verb/noun format—the action followed by the object of that action. For example, describe a data entry activity as "enter data" rather than "data entry." This approach keeps your map action oriented.

Each Post-it should be placed in the correct swim lane for the function involved, immediately to the right of the preceding action. The only Post-its that should be lined up vertically are those in which the tasks are being performed simultaneously (parallel activities). All other steps should be depicted serially from left to right. Later, a timeline will be added to the bottom of the map.

The following mapping tips will help the team move as quickly as possible through the first pass:

■ Encourage team members to view the process from the perspective of the *thing* (the work product) being passed through the process. The thing could be data, information, paperwork, drawings, equipment,

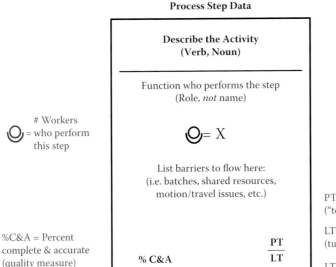

Figure 4.1 Post-it conventions.

material—or in the case of healthcare and other service environments, it might be a person. In some cases, the thing experiences the process from a stationery position, such as a patient in an emergency room or equipment being serviced. Regardless of whether the thing is moving or stationery, if team members pretend they are the thing experiencing the process ("*be the thing*" is a common reminder), they are less likely to skip over relevant process steps.

■ During this first pass in the MBPM process, the facilitator's most common question is: "And then what happens?" The team's typical response is: "It depends." To minimize the "it depends" responses, which slow the mapping process, you may need to further refine the target process beyond the specific conditions defined when you scoped the mapping activity. At this level of detail, you should map only one or two specific conditions, and then design the future-state to accommodate a broader set of circumstances. For example, your original scope may have been to analyze a process that is performed in a particular region for a national company, or a specific time of the year when volume is greatest. When creating the MBPM, the team may have to refine the scope further and focus on a particular customer group or type of service being delivered.

■ Regardless of the specific process you end up mapping, create a map that reflects what happens during 80 percent of the occurrences.

In some cases, it can be helpful for the team to focus on a specific example as a point of reference. You want to focus on the norm, not the outliers and exceptions. Exceptions often seem more frequent than reality because they are typically more painful to deal with, so teams often focus on those situations. To avoid slowing the mapping process, the facilitator will need to keep reminding the team to focus on *the 80 percent*. In the case of large swings in process time or lead time, it can be helpful to ask the team to determine the shortest time and the longest time. From there, it is often easier for them to ignore the outliers and agree on a number that fits 80 percent of the time. If the exceptions are causing the greatest pain and are what need to be addressed, then those exceptions are fair game for improvement and should be targeted when the mapping activity is being scoped.

■ Since this is a time-based map (the clock is ticking continuously from the first to the last step), you'll need to "serialize" the process steps, in sequence from left to right, including those that typically loop. For example, if the thing passing through the system is sent back to an upstream supplier for correction 90 percent of the time, depict each of those steps serially on the map. Place three Post-its in sequence to depict the rework cycle: (1) initial receipt/review of the work product by the customer, (2) correction of the error by the upstream supplier, and (3) processing of the corrected work product by the customer.

■ While the team members are initially documenting the current state, they will be tempted to begin designing improvements. To keep the team fully focused on the current state, the facilitator should record their improvement suggestions on a flip chart or whiteboard, and guide their attention back to the current state as quickly as possible. Don't let the team get distracted and start evaluating ideas at this stage; that comes later.

■ Creating the current-state MBPM is eye opening, but it can be tedious work. The facilitator should keep the team members' energy up by regularly applauding their efforts, acknowledging that it is hard work, and assuring them that there will be payoff when they begin designing the future state.

■ Mapping teams nearly always benefit by performing a *gemba walk* or *going to the gemba* (also referred to as genchi genbutsu)—going to where the work is actually performed to observe the process in action. This is particularly helpful for high-volume, repetitive processes that have a relatively short total process time. Going to the gemba enables mapping teams to gain greater clarity about the work environment, assess the degree of work in process (WIP) and queuing present, witness work being performed, begin engaging a broader cross section of the workforce in thinking about process design, asking why work is done a certain way, and so on. It's tempting, but extremely risky, to map the process solely from the confines of a conference room. A team focused on making improvement will often gain valuable insights and observe obvious waste that they themselves didn't notice prior to the mapping activity.

Another option is to *bring the gemba* to the mapping team. For some processes, workers can demonstrate process steps in a conference room as effectively as they can at the gemba, which may be logistically challenging to arrange, or where a mapping team may be too intrusive for the particular work environment. For example, in some cases team members can demonstrate the transactions they perform on a computer connected to an LCD (liquid crystal display) projector.

Second Pass: Add Key Metrics for Each Step, Create the Timeline, and Calculate the Summary Metrics

Next, the team adds the three key metrics for analyzing and monitoring a process—lead time (LT), process time (PT), and percent complete and accurate (%C&A). Most of this data is obtained by questioning the relevant process workers. Keep in mind that you want to obtain *directionally correct* data; that is, the data needs to be accurate enough to result in solid conclusions and relevant decisions regarding prioritization. You don't need to conduct operational research and measure with high degrees of precision to achieve these objectives. During the second pass, with its different focus, the team often discovers a few missing steps, which should be added to create a more accurate map.

The Excel documentation tool on the accompanying CD includes a summary sheet that defines the key mapping metrics (eighth tab). It is helpful to share this sheet with the team either during the Lean overview training or during mapping. It is important that the team fully understand the three key metrics—lead time, process time, and percent complete and accurate—before the facilitator leads them into this phase. For teams new to Lean terminology and these metrics, the facilitator will likely need to keep reminding them about the difference between process time and lead time. The three key metrics are determined as described below.

Process Time

Process time (PT) is the actual time it takes a worker to perform a task if he or she could work on it uninterrupted and all waiting and delays were removed from the process. In addition to the time spent *touching* the work, process time includes the *talk time* for clarification or obtaining additional information to perform the task—or anything else that occupies a worker's time and attention to the point that he or she cannot work on something else. Process time also includes the *think time* required to perform a task if analysis and/or review is involved.

In office and service settings, process time is often expressed in minutes or hours and is typically obtained by interviewing the people who actually do the work rather than conducting time/motion studies or other elaborate forms of obtaining exact measurements. If true measurements (not desired standards) are relatively easy to obtain, accuracy beats approximation any day. But remember, you only need data that is directionally correct enough to draw accurate conclusions and make effective decisions. If scientifically obtained data would not alter your conclusions or affect your decisions, there's little point in taking the time to obtain it.

As indicated in Figure 4.1, the preferred mapping convention is to place process time in the lower right corner of the Post-it, above the line that separates it from lead time. *Note:* The facilitator will also need to keep team members moving along and help them realize that if the lead time is four hours for a particular step (four hours from the work being made available until it is completed and passed on to the next person or department), it does not matter if a task takes 5 minutes or 7 minutes. Either number will illustrate the delay that exists and will provide a good enough baseline from which to measure improvement. Teams often get hung up on perfection. It is the facilitator's job to explain why, in mapping, debating a few minutes that occur over the course of many hours is not as important as is completing the map so the team can get to its key mission: designing and implementing an improved process.

Lead Time

Lead time (LT) is the elapsed time from the moment work is made available to a particular worker or team, until it has been completed *and made available* to the next person or team in the process. Lead time equals process time plus waiting and delays, and is usually expressed in hours or days. Lead time is also usually obtained by interviewing the people who *currently* perform the work being analyzed.

As shown in Figure 4.1, LT is placed below the horizontal line in the lower right corner of the Post-it. For both PT and LT, always include the units of measure—mins or M, hours or H, and so on.

When presenting the current-state findings, it is helpful to express lead time in a unit of measure greater than the process time. So, if your lead time is most easily expressed in weeks, your process time might be expressed in days or hours. If your lead time is in hours, your process time might be expressed in minutes or seconds. This technique makes the waste far more obvious (e.g., why does it take eight hours to complete only five minutes of work?), especially when the lead time is significantly longer than the process time. It's also easier for people to quickly grasp small numbers—e.g., 6 hours versus 360 minutes.

With particularly complicated processes, it is sometimes helpful to determine lead time in chunks, rather than include it for each and every step. (The same is not true for process time, however.) If a series of steps occurs in any given department before a handoff to another department, you can obtain the typical lead time for the series of steps, rather than breaking it into individual components. For extremely long total lead times (i.e., weeks or months), you may want to assess lead time for large chunks of activities. For example, a 3-week lead time may reside in one area for 2 business days, another for 8 business days, and a third for 5 business days. If you break the map into segments, place the segment lead time on the last Post-it for that segment and leave the area below the line blank for all other steps (or place a "0").

When using MBPM to map a single block on a value stream map (VSM), it is fairly common to find that, when the MBPM is complete, the metrics do not match those on the corresponding VSM block(s). This occurs because the MBPM is a finer analytical tool and gets into the process "nooks and crannies." If the numbers are far off, reconcile the differences and adjust the corresponding VSM values, if needed.

Percent Complete and Accurate

Percent complete and accurate (%C&A), which reflects the quality of each process step's output, is obtained by interviewing downstream users (customers) of the upstream supplier's output and asking them what percentage of the time they can do their work without having to do any of the following forms of rework:

- Correct the information that was provided.
- Add missing information that should have been supplied.
- Clarify information that should have been clearer.

As shown in Figure 4.1, the %C&A should be recorded on the lower left corner on the Post-it for the step that *produced* the output, not the Post-it for the downstream customer who you received it. A %C&A of 80 percent on a particular process step means that the downstream customer has to correct, add, or clarify (CAC) about 20 percent of the time.

If the same individual performs a number of sequential steps before handing off to the next person in the process, it may be difficult to pinpoint which specific step contributed to the %C&A. In this case, you may attribute the %C&A to the last step in the sequence (the one where the output's being handed off) and assume all preceding steps for that sequence are 100 percent.

Occasionally, a worker may generate output with a low %C&A that is not detected by the immediate customer, but rather, is apparent to customers farther downstream. In this case, you go back to the Post-it for the step producing the output and note each observed %C&A, along with an indication of which step number is detecting the quality issue.

Determining %C&A can sometimes make the worker who generated the low %C&A uncomfortable to learn that his or her output has not been meeting the internal customers' needs. But, with proper facilitation and a blame-free environment, these discoveries can be positive and provide the trigger for necessary dialogue between internal customers and suppliers regarding expectations and requirements.

Additional Information

As depicted in Figure 4.1, you may also want to document any significant barriers to flow the team has identified and the number of employees available to perform the work in question. Significant barriers included batched work, system downtime, shared resources, or anything else that prevents work from flowing through the step or to the next step without delay. You may also want to note the number of employees who are available to perform the work, especially if you sense that you may need to balance workloads, shift work from one person to another, or segment different types of work. The circle with a curved line below it is an icon borrowed from value stream mapping and represents an aerial view of a person sitting in a chair.

Timeline Critical Path

At this point, you should have a map that includes a Post-it for each step of the process being analyzed. Each Post-it should include a brief description of the activity taking place, as well as three key metrics: PT, LT, and %C&A. Keeping in mind that *lead time* is a critical metric in the Lean approach, your map will need to reflect the total elapsed time from the moment a request is made until a product or service has been delivered. Defining the timeline critical path allows you to determine the overall lead time for the entire process.

So, at this stage, you need to review your MBPM. Does it contain parallel steps (work that is being performed in two areas simultaneously)? If so, you'll need to determine which of the concurrent activities comprises the critical path. If the team has constructed the map properly, parallel activities will be depicted as two or more Post-its aligned vertically (directly above or below one another), which illustrates that they are being performed concurrently. In other words, Post-its aligned vertically should depict activities that occur more or less within the same timeframe as the process's ticking clock continues.

Typically, the steps that belong to the timeline critical path are those with the longest lead times. But first you need to eliminate from consideration any of the parallel steps that lead to a *dead end* in the process—that is, there is no output from the step (e.g., filing paperwork that's not accessed again, calling a customer to inform them of status, etc.). These parallel steps are not part of the timeline critical path, no matter how long their lead times are. Once you have eliminated the dead-end steps, review the remaining parallel steps, and select those in the sequence with the longest collective lead time.

Figure 4.2 represents a segment of an MBPM for a quoting process. Within this segment there are three parallel paths, or sequences, of activities. In determining the timeline critical path, the top row is eliminated since it dead-ends at filing. Of the two remaining sequences of parallel activities, the finance function becomes the timeline critical path since its collective lead time is longer than the collective lead time of the legal function (seven days versus four days). In this example, the bold curved line indicates the timeline critical path.

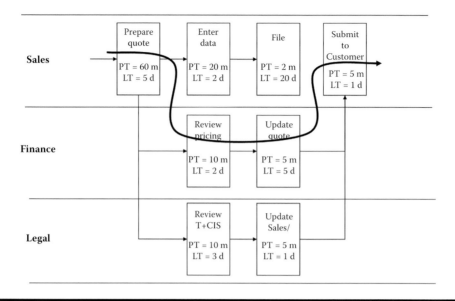

Figure 4.2   Critical path determination.

You can visually depict the timeline critical path in a number of ways. We typically use a brightly colored marker (e.g., red) and draw the timeline critical path across the entire MBPM as shown in Figure 4.2. There are other options as well. The key is to make the timeline critical path visually apparent. *Mapping tip:* Make sure your map is 100 percent complete before you determine the timeline critical path.

To create the timeline, draw a horizontal line across the bottom of your map. (*Note:* You may need to hang additional paper for this.) Label the line with "PT" and "LT" and the appropriate units of measure as shown in Figure 4.3. Place the process times for the corresponding critical path steps directly below the corresponding process steps and directly above the line you just drew (in the numerator position). Place the lead times for the corresponding critical path steps just below the line (in the denominator position).

Summary Metrics

Once the map is complete, all of the steps contain the three key metrics (PT, LT, and %C&A), and the critical path has been determined, it is time to calculate the summary metrics for the current-state MBPM as follows (see the eighth tab on the Excel tool on the CD for a summary document.

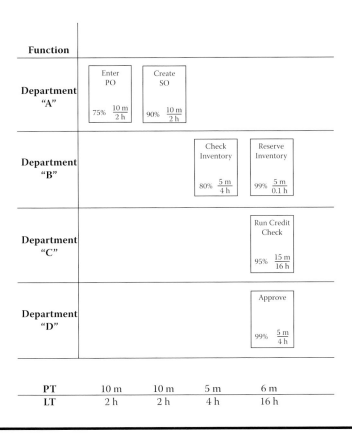

Figure 4.3   MBPM with summary timeline.

Timeline Critical Path (CP) Summation

Add *together* the individual timeline critical path PTs and LTs. Place the totals to the right of the timeline as summations (Σ). Validate the total CP LT with objective data, or a "gut check" if objective data is not available. Does the total CP LT match the team's experience of how much time generally elapses from the beginning to the end of the process? If it does not match objective data or the team's experience, review the LTs for the individual steps or process segments, and revise if necessary. Convert the CP PT and LT to the same unit of measure in preparation for the calculated metrics phase, described later in this section.

Rolled Percent Complete and Accurate (R%C&A)

Multiply together the %C&As for all process steps (not just the critical path). This quality metric tells you how many "things" out of 100 experience the process with no quality issues—no need to correct, add, or clarify information provided by an upstream supplier. In other words, they pass through the process "clean" with no rework required. The current-state R%C&A is often shockingly low. And if the %C&A at any process step is 0 percent (a surprisingly common finding), the R%C&A for the entire process will naturally be 0 percent. In the example in Figure 4.3, the R%C&A is 50%. Fifty percent of the work items passing through this process experience rework at some point.

Activity Ratio (AR)

Also referred to as percent activity (% activity), this metric indicates the magnitude of the opportunity for improvement in the flow of work through a process. Expressed as a percentage, it reflects the ratio of the time "the thing" going through the process is being worked on versus the time it sits around waiting. To calculate the AR, convert your timeline critical path PT and LT to the same units of measure (e.g., hours, days, etc). Then divide the sum of the timeline critical path PTs by the sum of the timeline critical path LTs and multiply by 100:

$$\text{Activity Ratio} = \frac{\Sigma \text{ Timeline Critical Path PT}}{\Sigma \text{ Timeline Critical Path LT}} \times 100$$

Two notes of caution: In office environments, the current-state activity ratio is often quite low—in the 5–15 percent range—which indicates ample opportunity for improvement. Naturally, you would like to get as close to 100 percent as possible—true flow. But this is often difficult to achieve in office environments due to high degrees of switchtasking. So for the first few rounds of improvement, we recommend that you focus on your degree of improvement rather than the actual numbers. If, for example, your current-state activity ratio is 3 percent, designing a future-state activity ratio of 6 percent is a 100 percent projected improvement that should be celebrated. Naturally, this number also indicates the tremendous need for ongoing improvement.

Second, be aware that those who are new to measurement can be misled by the activity ratio. In the initial efforts to improve an office process, you may find that the activity ratio actually drops. But this is not necessarily a bad thing. Remember, it is a *ratio*, expressed as a percentage. If you improve both the PT and the LT but the percent improvement for the PT is greater than the percent improvement for the LT, the postimprovement ratio will be lower than the preimprovement baseline measurement. But reducing both the LT and the PT is a success that should be celebrated. LT and PT reductions are, after all, your ultimate goal. Make sure you enlighten team members and leadership to this fact so they understand that, although the AR may have decreased, the team has made meaningful improvements.

Number of Steps

Count the total number of Post-its (include all of the parallel steps).

Total Process Time

Total process is the sum of the process time for all steps (not just the time-line critical path). This metric is used when calculating labor (full-time equivalents or FTEs) requirements and determining the freed capacity that the improvement is projected to create.

Mapping tip: It is best to depict the total PT in the units of measure that are the easiest to comprehend. So, even if you have captured each individual process step in minutes, you may want to express the total PT in hours or days. For example, 22.3 hours or 2.8 days is more easily understood than 1,338 minutes. And 1.5 days is easier to comprehend that 0.3 business weeks.

Also, if you use days as a unit of measure, make sure you specify whether it is calendar days or business days. For example, four calendar days may equal two business days, if a weekend is sandwiched between the days during which the process is worked. Most Monday through Friday operations work about 22 business days per month. If you are mapping a process in a 7-day-per-week operation such as law enforcement or inpatient hospital services, you will likely want to measure the process in calendar days.

Full-Time Equivalent (FTE) Labor Requirements

FTE is a measure of the labor effort or the staff required to execute the process if they were all full-time, and generally assumes a 40-hour work week. For example: 2 people, each working 20 hours per week, is equivalent to one FTE. It is helpful to measure the current-state FTE requirements for two reasons. First, it can be used to compare current-state staffing requirements according to the map versus actual staffing levels.* Second, the FTE calculation provides a baseline from which you can measure freed capacity created from future-state improvements that reduce process time.

To calculate FTE requirements, first add together the PTs for *all* of the process steps, not just the timeline critical path steps. Convert the PT sum into hours if it is not already. Multiply the PT sum by the number of occurrences per year (customer demand) and divide by the average number of available work hours to complete the work being studied.

$$\text{FTE Requirements} = \frac{\sum \text{PT in hours} \times \text{\# occurrences}}{\text{Available work hours per employee per year}}$$

The available work hours per employee per year is typically calculated by beginning with 2,080 (the typical number of *paid* work hours per year) and subtracting from it the number of paid holidays and median number of paid vacation days across the company. The resulting *available work hours per employee per year* typically ranges from 1,725 to 1,950. If your company only pays for 35 hours per week, then you begin with 1,820 (35 hours per week × 52 weeks per year). We don't typically subtract paid sick days, meeting and training time, or other activities that occupy workers' attention. A coarse measurement is good enough.

Other Relevant Metrics

Depending on the team's improvement focus, other metrics may be meaningful, such as:

- **Productivity:** Productivity is the number of units processed per person per unit of time (best used in high-volume, repetitive environments where staff is dedicated to a specific process).
- **Distance walked:** Distance walked is often used in conjunction with a spaghetti diagram. Distance walked measurements are useful for illustrating the cost and productivity impact of unnecessary walking, the benefits of colocating people, equipment, or supplies (often used in creating the business case for purchasing additional equipment),

---

* This comparison is only valid when the staff responsibilities are limited to the work being mapped. If staff members have other responsibilities that you have not mapped, you may not know what percentage of their time focuses on performing the mapped process versus their other responsibilities.

and the benefits of eliminating hand-walking for approvals, input, or work expedition.

- **Morale:** Measuring morale is relevant when seeking to improve levels of engagement, reduce stress and absenteeism, reduce turnover, and so on.
- **Customer satisfaction:** Customer satisfaction is useful in any improvement effort, but especially relevant when seeking to reduce customer complaints. The two key components of customer satisfaction are: (1) quality received and (2) percentage of on-time delivery (based on customer expectation and need).
- **Overall equipment effectiveness (OEE):** This metric is particularly useful when assessing how effectively capital-intensive and/or revenue-producing equipment is being utilized, such as medical equipment in healthcare or printing presses in the publishing industry. OEE is also helpful in demonstrating the reliability of non-revenue-producing equipment that impacts productivity, such as computers, law enforcement equipment, and so on.

Third Pass: Classify the Steps as Value-Adding and Necessary Non-Value-Adding

Once the mapping team has documented the current state and calculated the relevant metrics, their next step is to identify waste in the process—the unnecessary non-value-adding activities that become the team's target for elimination. The fastest way to accomplish this is to first identify the *value-adding* steps in the process, followed by the *necessary* non-value-adding steps (also referred to as *essential work* or *value-enabling activities*). All remaining activities are considered waste—those activities that your external customer (the end user of the services provided and goods produced) does not value; by extension, is not willing to pay for; and are not essential for running the business. In processes where customers or end users don't pay for the goods or services they receive (as is sometimes found in government, healthcare, and social services)—or they only pay a small portion toward the total cost—the team needs to analyze each activity as though the customer were paying fully for the services they receive.

In many environments, a secondary external customer also exists—an intermediate party that pays directly for goods and services, controls access to the goods or services, or initiates a process on an end user's behalf.

Healthcare, distribution networks, and subcontracting relationships represent a few examples of this. When primary and secondary external customers coexist, the mapping team should differentiate between value-adding and non-value-adding activities by first viewing the process from the end user or primary customer's perspective. After they've made that determination, they can review the process once more from the secondary customer's perspective. The reason why they don't view the process only from the perspective of the secondary customer (who is typically closest to the process, and therefore could be erroneously viewed as a better arbiter of value) is that they will typically uncover more waste when they view a process from the end user's perspective.

You may be asking: What about *internal* customers? While considering internal customers' needs is a vital component of creating flow in a process, they are not the customer group used here to classify process steps as value-adding or non-value-adding. If internal customers require work that external customers would deem *unnecessary* non-value-adding, the team may classify the steps as necessary non-value-adding. But they should be extremely discriminating when making this determination to avoid including activities in the future-state design that should be eliminated.

As the team identifies the truly value-adding (VA) steps—which often comprise 10 percent or fewer of the process steps—a smaller Post-it with "VA" on it is placed below or next to the VA steps, as shown in Figure 4.4. Next, they will identify the necessary non-value-adding activities. Necessary non-value-adding activities are those that the external customer is not willing to pay for, but they are (1) essential for the organization to exist as a viable business entity or (2) essential for delivering value to the customer. You can think of this type of work as *value enabling*.

A smaller Post-it with "N" on it (a different color Post-it can be visually helpful) is placed below or next to the relevant steps. (*Mapping tip:* Post-its don't stick well to other Post-its, even the super-sticky type. So you should either affix the "VA" Post-it directly to the mapping paper or tape them to the larger Post-it to assure the VA labels remain affixed.) In the case of multiple external customers, the team may wish to affix VA and N labels in different colors to differentiate the various customer perspectives.

Next, the team should scan the map one more time to assure that all unlabeled steps are truly waste and are, therefore, targets for elimination.

Mapping tip: Some lean practitioners prefer to have their teams label every single step, but labeling only those that are value-adding and

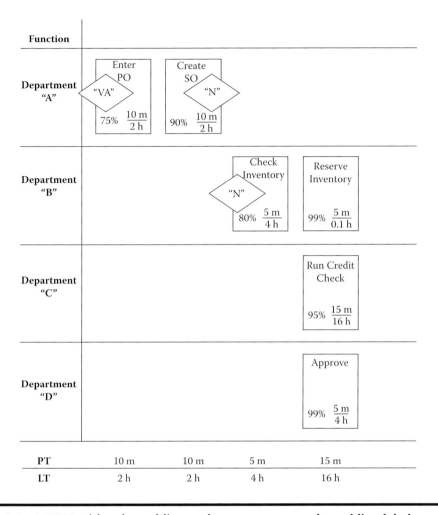

Figure 4.4 MBPM with value-adding and necessary non-value-adding labels.

necessary non-value-adding creates a stronger visual statement about the degree to which waste exists in the process and prevents the map from becoming cluttered with labels.

Once the team has identified which activities are value-adding, two additional metrics can be used to provide further understanding about the current state and set the stage for innovative future-state design: (1) percent value-adding in terms of time (%VA) and (2) percent value-add in terms of the process steps (%VA Steps). In most cases, neither of these metrics is used for ongoing measurement, but they are often helpful for illustrating the degree of waste, and therefore opportunity present in the current state.

◼ **Percent value-adding (%VA):** This value is calculated as follows: add together the individual process times for the all of the VA steps (do not include the N-labeled steps) in the timeline critical path and divide by the total lead time for the timeline critical path:

$$\%VA = \frac{\Sigma \text{ Timeline Critical Path PT for VA Steps}}{\Sigma \text{ Timeline Critical Path LT}} \times 100$$

Since a portion of a process's total process time is consumed by non-value-adding activities, the %VA is usually lower—often *significantly* lower—than the activity ratio described previously. And if you are analyzing a support process, during which no value is being provided from the discerning eyes of your primary external customer, it may be that %VA is 0 percent.

Some Lean practitioners prefer not to use this metric for support processes that are necessary to operate the business but do not deliver direct value to the customer for fear it will demotivate a team that has been charged with improving a process. But when discussed in a constructive manner, a 0 percent VA finding can drive improvement teams to be more innovative in their efforts to reduce waste than if they ignored the fact that none of the activities in the process are value-adding when viewed from an external customer's perspective. If they ignore a 0 percent VA finding, they also risk perpetuating the disconnect that often exists between internal support departments and external customers. For an organization to become a Lean enterprise, their internal support departments need to be thinking as much about external customers as are those who provide direct value.

◼ **%VA steps:** Count the number of VA steps and divide by the total number of steps in the process (including all parallel activities) to determine what percentage of the steps themselves include value-adding activities.

$$\%VA \text{ Steps} = \frac{\#VA \text{ Steps}}{\text{Total } \# \text{ Steps}} \times 100$$

Again, this metric is not typically used for ongoing process monitoring, but it is often a powerful stimulant for change when a team finds that, for example, only 3 out of 25 steps add value.

With the VA and N steps now identified, the final activity during the third pass is to highlight the process steps that contain the greatest waste and are the largest contributors to the process performance issue(s) that are driving the improvement effort. Examples might include long lead times (especially in proportion to the process time), poor quality (low %C&A), overprocessing (all of the steps not labeled as VA or N), and other barriers to flow such as batching. Long process times are also relevant because reducing process time reduces lead time and improves productivity. If one of the event objectives is to free capacity so the organization can absorb additional work without increasing staffing by its usual proportions, targeting long process times becomes especially relevant. Look at *all* process steps to make this determination. Some of the greatest opportunities to make improvements may lie in the value-adding and necessary non-value-adding steps.

The team can visually highlight the greatest waste in any number of ways: by putting a specific colored Post-it above the relevant process step, by circling the step or the improvement-worthy metric with a brightly colored marker, or by turning the Post-it on its side. The key is creating a clear visual that helps the team as it moves into future-state design.

At this point, the team members are typically clear about where the waste is in the process. But in many cases, they still do not know *why* it exists. So, before team members begin the future-state design process, they often need to dig a little deeper and uncover the root cause behind the waste they have identified. The root causes that team members uncover will prove to be the true target for elimination rather than the waste itself, which is merely a symptom of an underlying problem.

If the improvement team fails to "peel back the layers of the onion" to reveal the true root cause of waste, it risks creating two undesirable outcomes: (1) designing suboptimal solutions that only treat the symptoms or only partially resolve the problem and (2) designing solutions that resolve the problem short term, but allow waste to creep back into the process because the root cause hasn't been fully eliminated. Without proper root-cause analysis, the team risks jumping to conclusions or creating Band-Aid® fixes. The four basic tools for root-cause analysis include:

- The Five Whys
- Cause-and-effect diagrams
- Checklists
- Pareto charts

If you are unfamiliar with these tools, there are many books, websites, and workshops that you can attend to learn about how to conduct robust root-cause analysis.

Once you've uncovered the true root cause(s) for the waste you've identified, you're ready to create and implement the future state you've designed, the subject of Chapter 5.

Chapter 5

Mapping Essentials: Designing and Implementing the Future State

Once the team has uncovered the root causes for the waste that exists, they are ready to design the future state and the implementation plan to achieve it. Improvements should focus on reducing lead time, reducing process time (which is often a by-product of reducing the lead time), and improving the quality of the output produced in each of the remaining steps.

You can create the future-state map on a fresh segment of paper and new Post-its® or you may prefer modifying the current-state map to reflect the future state. If we anticipate that the future-state map will be significantly different from the current state, we typically begin with fresh paper (but we may cut it a bit shorter to send a visual message that the future-state map will likely have fewer steps/Post-its). Not only do most future-state maps include fewer steps, many include fewer functions (swim lanes) as well.

The mapping conventions for creating the future-state Metrics-Based Process Mapping (MBPM) are the same as those for documenting the current state, with a few small differences. Some teams like to depict changes to the process with different colored Post-its. Some teams prefer using *Kaizen bursts* to visually depict the planned improvements (which form the basis for the implementation plan discussed later in this chapter). The other difference is that, until the improvements are designed, implemented, and measured, the summary metrics are *projected*. Once the process metrics have stabilized, they can be referred to as *postimprovement* metrics.

But, before you attempt to project how the improved process will perform, you need to determine the specific methods you'll use—the *countermeasures*—to eliminate the root cause(s) for the waste you identified in the current state.

Selecting Countermeasures

Designing the future state for a process is where experience pays off and where a seasoned facilitator is necessary. Team members new to improvement won't necessarily be familiar with the variety of *countermeasures* available to them that can be used to eliminate the root causes for waste, and improve process quality, speed, and flow. For the best results, your facilitator needs to be highly proficient using the full range of countermeasures for eliminating waste.

We prefer the term *countermeasure* over *solution* because the term solution implies permanence, which runs counter to the concept of continuous improvement. A solution smacks of something you put in place and then move on to the next problem. But even highly relevant and well-executed "solutions" are temporary; processes need to be continuously adjusted to accommodate changing conditions. While countermeasure may sound clinical or even militaristic, it is a more accurate term, linguistically, for what you're actually doing during the course of improvement: countering an existing problem. Avoiding the term solutions helps set more realistic expectations and builds the mental framework you need to build a continuous improvement culture.

So which countermeasures will you need to implement to realize your future state? Two words: it depends. Countermeasures are not tools to be applied without deep thought. They are highly situational depending on the type of waste you find in the current state, the root cause(s) for the waste, the objectives of the improvement activities, and the host of process and environmental variables at play. But we can give some rough guidance.

First, it helps to remember that you're seeking to eliminate three conditions that are detrimental to customers, the business itself, and its employees: mura (waste), muri (overburden on employees and machines), and mura (inconsistencies and unevenness around demand and how work is performed). The facilitator should be familiar with and proficient at identifying the eight common types of waste: overproduction, inventory, overprocessing, waiting, errors, motion, transportation, and underutilization of people (often referred to as *lost creativity*), and should transfer his or her knowledge to the team.

Once the root cause(s) for waste, overburden, and inconsistencies are clearly identified, it's easier to know which countermeasures are appropriate. Nearly all processes benefit by standardizing work (to the degree it makes sense for the specific process being improved) to reduce variation in output quality and the time it takes to complete work. Standardization provides more predictable outcomes, which aids in planning, decision making, work management, making customer commitments, and the like. (*Note:* It can sometimes take an organization *years* just to create standard work for its major processes.)

The benefits of standardization go far beyond creating a baseline from which to measure improvement. Effective decision making relies on a degree of predictability. Without predictable process performance, it's difficult for leadership to have high degrees of confidence that the decisions they're making will have the desired impact. It's equally difficult to train new employees if processes aren't well defined and well documented. Finally, we've found that interpersonal and interdepartmental tension results primarily from poorly defined and managed processes rather than personality or turf issues. When cross-functional teams come together to standardize the work they do, the tension that typically develops from poor-quality inputs or outputs, or delays in the process, frequently resolves in one or two meetings.

In the process of standardizing work, other countermeasures are often implemented as well. For example, if quality problems are detected, error reduction techniques are implemented. If the process is production oriented and work is unbalanced, work balancing via takt time can produce better flow. If WIP (work in process or queuing) commonly accumulates, batch reduction, work balancing, pull systems, and level loading may prove helpful. To reduce motion, colocation is a potential countermeasure. If the workforce is underutilized, creating multifunctional workers may provide relief. And so on.

It bears repeating: The key for knowing which countermeasure(s) will produce the results you desire is to clearly identify the current state and the root cause(s) for it to begin with. Not knowing which countermeasure to apply is often the result of ambiguity about the root cause for the problem at hand or lack of experience with process improvement.

Once you know the specific improvements you need to make, the next step is to create an implementation plan that outlines how you'll execute improvement to realize the future state.

Implementing the Future State

Once the future-state map is created, root causes have been identified, and countermeasures have been selected, it's time to create an implementation plan. You may create your own or use the one we've provided on tab 7 on the Excel Tool (Figure 5.1).

The Goal/Objective column houses the specific target metrics that will serve as the means for assessing whether the process is performing as desired or not. The Improvement Activity column lists the countermeasure that will be implemented as well as any additional details that may be needed.

Mode is the type of activity that will be undertaken to implement the countermeasures, whether a Kaizen Event (KE), traditional project (PROJ), or a "just do it (JDI)," an improvement that can be made in a matter

Metrics-Based Process Mapping
Future State Implementation Plan

		Implementation Plan Review Dates	
Process Name			
Executive Sponsor			
Process Owner			
Mapping Facilitator			
Date Created			

Step #	Goal / Objective	Improvement Activity	Mode*	Owner	Implementation Schedule (weeks)												Date Complete
					1	2	3	4	5	6	7	8	9	10	11	12	

Approvals		
Executive Sponsor	Process Owner	Mapping Facilitator
Signature:	Signature:	Signature:
Date:	Date:	Date:

* Mode = JDI (Just-do-it), KE (Kaizen Event), PROJ (Project), or RPE (Rapid Planning Event)

Figure 5.1 Future-state implementation plan.

of hours and one that doesn't require a cross-functional team's input or buy-in. The Owner is the person who's accountable for seeing that the specific improvement on that row is successfully implemented and leading continuous improvement efforts if adjustment is needed. This may or may not be the same person as the Process Owner.

You can use the free-form arrows that are found to the right of the map to complete the Implementation Schedule section, shrinking or expanding them to depict the planned start and end points for the defined improvements.

Plans that will take more than a week or so to fully execute should be reviewed every week or two by whomever is overseeing the improvement effort—ideally, the process owner, if one has been named—and an improvement team (if one has been assembled) or the people closest to the work being improved (if no improvement team exists).

Once the full implementation plan has been executed and any adjustments to the process that may be needed are made, your future state is fully realized and has become the new current state. And then a new Plan-Do-Study-Adjust (PDSA) improvement cycle begins.

As you're approaching the end of the first improvement cycle, you'll need to decide whether archiving the map in electronic form is warranted. Remember, once you implement all of the countermeasures you've identified, the improved process should be viewed as the new standard work that's used by all new hires to learn how to perform their jobs and by all managers to monitor and improve the process on an ongoing basis.

Read on to learn how to document the new standard work by using the Excel tool provided on the CD in the back of this book.

Chapter 6

Process Documentation: An Excel-Based Solution

As we mentioned in Chapter 5, once all of the planned improvements have been implemented, the Metrics-Based Process Mapping (MBPM) serves as the standard work that's used to train new hires on the process, as well as to monitor process performance and drive continuous improvement. After we developed the mapping technique and began deploying it at our clients, they began asking us for the means to electronically document the manual maps their teams had created using paper and Post-it® notes. They understandably wanted an easy way to share the new standard work they had created with staff in remote locations. They also wanted a concise way to teach new hires the steps in the process and the accompanying process performance expectations, and help them see how their specific role fits into the larger cross-functional picture.

Little did we know when we created our initial rudimentary tool that it would evolve into a multilayered mapping tool that includes features such as automatic color coding to depict the timeline critical path, a summary report that autocalculates, and error-proofing features. As time went on, we incorporated a mapping charter, and now, in this release, an implementation plan.

The Excel tool, which does not require you to have extensive Excel experience, provides not only the means to visually represent the current and improved process flows, but it also autocalculates key metrics that reflect the quantifiable benefits of the improved state. However—and this is a critical point—it is intended to be used *after, not in lieu of* a cross-functional team manually creating an MBPM using butcher/plotter paper and

Post-its. It's intended as a tool for training and monitoring your new way of operating, not the means for process analysis. To achieve the greatest benefits from Metrics-Based Process Mapping, we strongly recommend you do not skip the manual mapping process and map directly into the Excel tool—even if it's being projected onto a screen. Creating electronic versions of manually produced maps proves helpful when

- you wish to archive a team's work
- you need to distribute the map electronically
- the map will serve as a standard work document, training tool, and/or analytical tool for process monitoring and continuous improvement.

Due to the detailed nature of an MBPM, digital photos are not sufficient as a means for archiving and distributing the map electronically. However, in the spirit of eliminating redundancies and rework, be judicious when deciding whether you need to convert manually created maps into electronic form, and only do so if the electronic version is necessary and will be well utilized.

This chapter is organized into four sections that describe the step-by-step process for converting your manually produced map into the Excel tool. The first section provides general information that you should read *before you open the tool*. The second section invites you to *view* the mapping tool as you learn about its overall structure and functionality. The third section is structured as a learn–do module so you can "test drive" the tool and *create a sample map*. The final section provides miscellaneous map management and troubleshooting information. If you're a seasoned Excel user, you may wish to review Appendix A for a Quick Start Guide. (The Quick Start Guide also appears as tab 10 on the Excel tool itself.) With that in mind, let's begin.

General Information

This section includes specific information you need to read *before you open the Excel file.*

File Storage

The first decision you need to make is where to store the master MBPM file. We recommend you store copies of the CD files in a designated folder on a hard/shared drive and place the physical CD somewhere for safekeeping. You might want to create an MBPM file folder to house the process-specific maps you will create. Another approach is to store the master file in a parent folder and create subfolders for each process you are improving so you can store specific improvement-related documents in one location. Consider the End User License Agreement (Figure 6.4) when developing your storage strategy. Once the designated location is determined, use Windows Explorer to drag the file from the CD to the desired file folder.

Excel Versions

The CD includes two versions of the Excel tool: one for those using Microsoft Office Excel 2003, the other for those using Microsoft Office Excel 2007 or 2010. While both files provide the same functionality, there are a variety of nuances related to formatting, macros, and saving files that differ. We strongly recommend using the file that corresponds with the version of Microsoft Office being used by the license holder. This chapter was written primarily for Microsoft Office Excel 2007 and 2010 users. Recognizing that there are differences in the commands and navigation between Excel 2003 and later versions of Excel, specific instructions for using Excel 2003 are contained in Appendix B. Neither version of the tool will function properly with Macintosh computers.

Enabling Macros

The tool has been designed to utilize macros—mini-programs within the file that execute a series of commands. Macros benefit the user by simplifying tool functionality and reducing opportunities for errors. *Failing to enable the macros will severely limit your ability to use the MBPM tool.*

Macros are enabled within the Trust Center.* To access the Trust Center, first click the Microsoft Office button (Figure 6.1). Select **Excel Options > Trust Center > Trust Center Settings > Macro Settings**. There are four Macro Settings that set your security level for all Excel files.

If you select Enable All Macros before the file is opened, the macros will run when the MBPM file is launched. If you select Disable All Macros with Notification, a notification will appear in the Excel ribbon

---

* See Appendix B for Excel 2003-specific instructions.

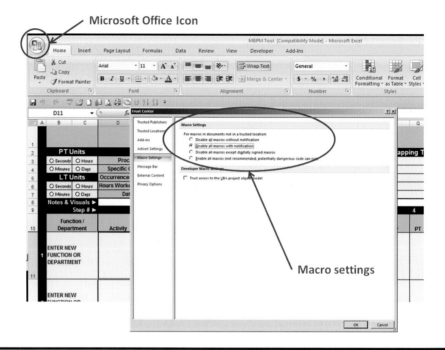

Figure 6.1   Macro setting options.

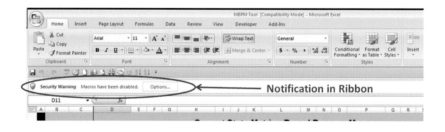

Figure 6.2   Macros-disabled notification.

(Figure 6.2). To enable macros, click **Options** and then select **Enable This Content**.

If you select either Disable All Macros without Notification or Disable All Macros Except Digitally Signed Macros, macros will not be enabled and the MBPM tool will not function properly. In this case, either change the Macro Settings option (see above) or contact your system administrator to have macros enabled for the MBPM tool.

If you attempt to use the custom toolbar (described in the next section) without enabling macros, you will receive one of a variety of pop-up windows, such as the one shown in Figure 6.3, indicating that Excel cannot find the macros necessary for the MBPM tool to function properly. Additional information regarding macro security is provided in the section "Excel Tool: Troubleshooting."

License Agreement

After you have enabled macros, you will receive a pop-up message that contains the End User License Agreement for this product (Figure 6.4). The license extends to a *single user only* for entering data into and/or editing and resaving the MBPM, but allows multiple employees within an organization to *view* completed MBPMs. In addition, all printed copies of the map must include the preprogrammed copyright notice in the footer. Additional copies of this book must be purchased to obtain additional licenses for the Excel tool.

Figure 6.3   Macros disabled error.

Figure 6.4   End User License Agreement.

To restrict unlicensed viewers' ability to create new or edit existing MBPMs, which violates the End User License Agreement, the custom toolbar should be locked prior to distribution (Figure 6.9). Select **Lock MBPM Custom Toolbar** from the **Map Management** drop-down menu and enter a password containing at least four numbers or letters. To unlock the toolbar, select **Unlock MBPM Custom Toolbar** from the **Map Management** drop-down menu and enter the password.

Another way to prevent unlicensed users from editing or creating maps is to use a PDF writer application (e.g., Adobe, PDF995 freeware, etc.) to convert the map from Excel to PDF format.

If you do not want the license agreement to appear each time you open the MBPM tool, check the box in the lower left corner. If you want to view the license, select **License Agreement** from the **Map Management** drop-down menu on the custom toolbar, as described in the next section.

File Saving Conventions

Beginning with Excel 2007, Microsoft introduced several new Excel file types. Since much of the tool functionality depends on the use of macros, it is critical that the file is saved as an Excel Macro-Enabled Workbook. The file extension for this file type is ".xlsm."

To Save a New Map from the Master File on the CD

Click the Microsoft Office button. Hover the mouse over **Save as**, and then click **Excel Macro-Enabled Workbook** from the options offered. In the **Save As** pop-up window, verify that the **Save as Type** is **Excel Macro-Enabled Workbook**. If the file type is incorrect, select **Excel Macro-Enabled Workbook** from the pull-down menu. Enter your preferred file name in the **File Name** field.

To Save a Map That Has Already Been Renamed and Saved as an Excel Macro-Enabled Workbook File Type

Either click the Save icon (looks like a floppy disk) on the Excel quick access tool bar or click the Microsoft Office button and select **Save**.

It bears repeating: For the Excel 2007 and 2010 MBPM tool to function properly, the file type must be ".xlsm." Failure to save the file in the correct format will result in a significant loss of functionality. *If at any point the tool is saved as a non-macro file type, the macros will be stripped from the file (a Microsoft safety feature) and you will need to recreate the map from scratch to regain functionality.*

File Naming Conventions

It's best to adopt a standard organizationwide file naming convention, such as including the acronym MBPM, the process name, and the mapping date in your file name—for example, "MBPM Custom Quotes 2012-05-28.xlsm." If you are creating a test map to practice with as you read this chapter, your file name could be "MBPM Test Map" or something similar.

Exiting the Tool

Because macros operate in the background, when you exit the tool, you will be asked whether you want to save changes or not, *even if you have not made any changes.* If you have made changes and want to save them, select **Yes**. If you have not made any changes to the file, or have made changes that you do not wish to save, select **No**. To be safe, we recommend that you always select **Yes** unless you expressly don't wish to save the changes you've made.

Structure and Features

This section provides an overview of the tool's structure and features. We recommend that you *view the tool only* as you read this section. We'll invite you to test drive the tool and create a sample map in the next section.

The MBPM tool contains a custom toolbar and ten sheets, accessed by selecting the tabs at the bottom of the Excel workspace. Let's take a look at each.

Custom Toolbar

Each time you open an MBPM file, a macro executes a command that adds a custom toolbar.* The custom toolbar is located in the Add-Ins tab (Figure 6.5). As shown in Figures 6.6, 6.7, 6.8, and 6.9, selecting any of

---

* See Appendix B for Excel 2003–specific instructions.

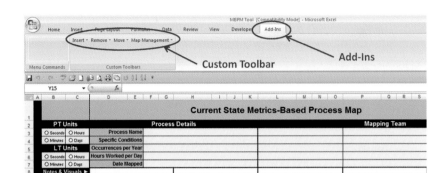

Figure 6.5   The custom toolbar.

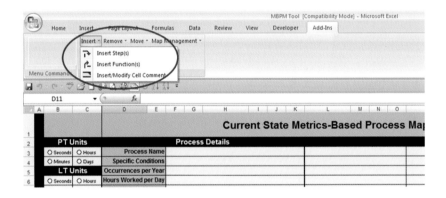

Figure 6.6   Custom toolbar: Insert drop-down menu.

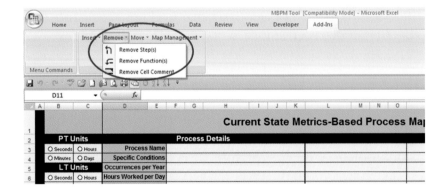

Figure 6.7   Custom toolbar: Remove drop-down menu.

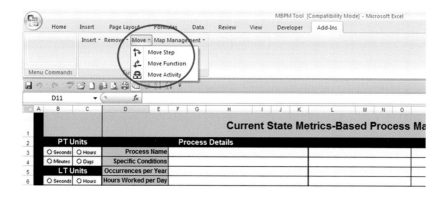

Figure 6.8   Custom toolbar: Move drop-down menu.

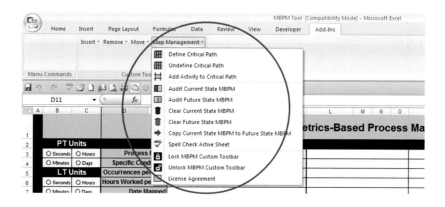

Figure 6.9   Custom toolbar: Map Management feature drop-down menu.

the toolbar's four options—Insert, Remove, Move, or Map Management—produces a drop-down menu of actions.

Notice that the drop-down menu for the Map Management feature includes 12 possible actions. If all 12 actions are not displayed, you may expand the list by clicking the downward arrow at the bottom of the list. Or, if you would like your drop-down lists to always display in full, you can alter your menu settings by choosing **Tools > Customize > Options** and check the **Always Show Full Menus** box.

The features on the custom toolbar are described in the next section. Table 6.1 lists the actions in alphabetical order and the pages on which the descriptions begin.

Table 6.1   Custom Toolbar Quick Reference Guide

Custom Toolbar Action	Page	Custom Toolbar Action	Page
Add Activity to Critical Path	72	License Agreement	53
Audit Current State MBPM	73	Lock Custom Toolbar	54
Audit Future State MBPM	73	Move Activity	68
Clear Current State MBPM	70	Move Function	67
Clear Future State MBPM	70	Move Step	67
Copy Current State MBPM to Future State MBPM	74	Remove Cell Comment	62
Define Critical Path	71	Remove Function(s)	66
Insert/Modify Cell Comment	62	Remove Step(s)	66
Insert Function(s)	65	Spell Check Active Sheet	70
Insert Step(s)	65	Undefine Critical Path	72
		Unlock Custom Toolbar	54

Worksheets

As shown in Figure 6.10 and described further in the following section, the tool is organized into ten worksheets accessed by tabs at the bottom of the Excel workspace:

1. **Current State:** This sheet is used to document the process as it was being performed at the time the process was mapped.
2. **Future State:** The newly designed process is documented on this sheet.
3. **Summary Metrics:** This sheet houses the before and after values for predefined performance metrics, capacity calculations, and user-defined metrics.
4. **Audit Findings:** Findings for the Audit Map feature on the Map Management section of the custom toolbar are listed on this sheet. The resulting messages include a list of various corrective actions you may need to take to ensure the Summary Metrics calculate accurately and a final congratulations message when your map meets all requirements. When you receive the congratulations message, the corresponding section on the Summary Metrics sheet autopopulates with the performance data.

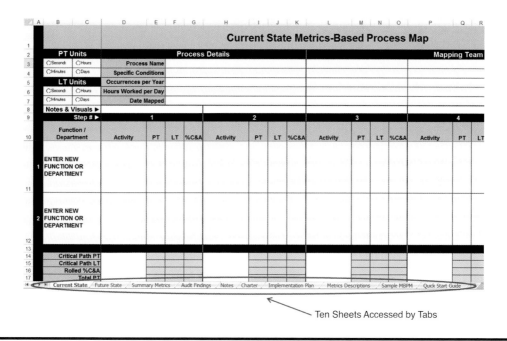

Figure 6.10   Ten sheets on the MBPM Excel tool.

5. **Notes:** This is a blank worksheet that can be used to record notes related to the maps, team, mapping process, and so on.

6. **Charter:** The charter, described in Chapter 3, serves as a planning and communication tool for the mapping activity.

7. **Implementation Plan:** The implementation plan can be used by those who are using the mapping tool in a more traditional project format.

8. **Metrics Descriptions:** This sheet lists and describes the key metrics that are found in the MBPM tool, including how they are calculated.

9. **Sample MBPM:** A sample current-state metrics-based process map is included to illustrate what a completed map typically looks like. You may find it helpful to take a look at the sample map before you read further.

10. **Quick Start Guide:** This is a greatly condensed version of this chapter.

Auto-Population Feature

As will be described fully in the next section, many of the sheets include cells that serve as source cells for the auto-population feature that is programmed into the MBPM tool. Cells that are salmon (tan) colored are programmed to auto-populate with data from source cells.

Map Structure

The Current State and Future State sheets are organized into three major sections, as shown in Figure 6.11:

■ **Header:** The header is organized into three subsections: PT and LT Units, Process Details, and Mapping Team, all of which are described in the Test-Driving section below. The Freeze Panes feature has been activated so that the process time (PT) and lead time (LT) units will always display on your screen.

■ **Body of the Map:** The body of the map includes the functions or departments involved in the process (listed vertically) and the steps (listed horizontally). Each process step is sequentially numbered and includes a description of the activity, the LT, PT, and percent complete and accurate (%C&A). These metrics are described on the Metrics Description sheet (Tab 8 of this tool) and in Chapter 4. The Freeze Panes feature has been activated so that the Function and Step labels will always display on your screen. In addition, row 8 is designed for user-defined content. Text can be placed in these cells or the cells can be colored coded.

■ **Step Summary:** Directly below each step are cells that contain relevant step-specific metrics—Critical Path PT, Critical Path LT, Rolled %C&A, and Total PT—all of which are described in Chapter 4. These cells serve as source data for many of the calculations that generate summary metrics.

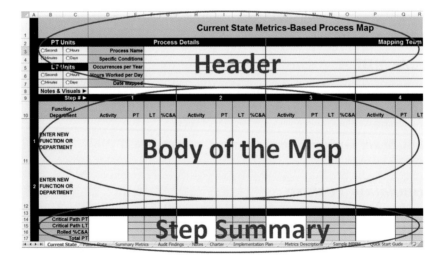

Figure 6.11   Three sections of the Excel tool.

Cell Colors

The cells on the Current State, Future State, Summary Metrics, and Audit Findings sheets are color-coded according to the cell's function, as shown in Table 6.2.

Cell Formatting

To prevent formatting errors, the size of all cells is fixed. When you enter more content than a cell's size allows, one of two actions takes place: (1) the text wraps within the cell, or (2) the font size automatically shrinks to accommodate the additional content, depending on the predefined format of the particular cell. When feasible, the text wrap feature was used. Since Excel does not limit how much text you can enter into a cell formatted to wrap text, if you enter a longer description than the cell can accommodate and the full description is not visible, you can take one of three actions:

1. Shorten your description.
2. Reduce the font size (click the cell to activate it, then right-click and select **Format Cell > Font > Size**).
3. Add a brief comment to house the overflow information by selecting the **Insert/Modify Cell Comment** option from the **Insert** drop-down menu on the custom toolbar. (See the description below regarding comment limitations.)

For those cells in which the tool layout would not accommodate text wrapping, the shrink-to-fit functionality was selected. In these cells, the font size will automatically reduce to the size necessary to fit all of the text into

Table 6.2 Cell Color-Coding Conventions

Cell Color	Design/Function
Yellow	These are the only cells that will accept direct data entry from the user.
Salmon (Tan)	These locked cells autopopulate, drawing on data that have been entered elsewhere in the tool or contain the results of predefined calculations. If the source data are modified, the salmon-colored cells update automatically or upon execution of the appropriate command.
Blue	As the user defines the timeline critical path cells containing timeline critical path activities and their associated metrics are color-coded blue.

the space available. If the font becomes too small, you may either reduce the amount of content or insert a comment as described previously to house the excess text. We encourage brevity, but not at the expense of clarity.

Insert, Modify, and Remove Comments

You may insert comments or modify existing comments by choosing **Insert/ Modify Cell Comment** on the custom toolbar's **Insert** feature. To remove comments, select **Remove > Remove Cell Comment** under the toolbar's **Remove** feature.

Enter Key Functionality

The Enter key functionality has been modified for use with this MBPM tool. Whereas Excel's default setting for the Enter key is vertical movement (i.e., pressing the Enter key advances the cursor *down* one cell), because the MBPM is a horizontally oriented tool, the Enter key has been programmed to advance the cursor to the *right*. The arrow keys may be used to navigate vertically on the tool.

Cut, Copy, and Paste Disabled

To ensure proper execution of macros and calculations, and to preserve the layout and look of the tool, Excel's cut, copy, and paste features have been disabled. Much of the functionality of these commands is provided to you through the remove, insert, move, and copy commands found in the custom toolbar.

Test-Driving the Tool: Documenting Current- and Future-State MBPMs

Before you take a test drive, you should familiarize yourself with the metrics and the corresponding acronyms used in Metrics-Based Process Mapping, which are listed on the Metrics Descriptions sheet and described fully in Chapter 4. You may want to print the Metrics Description sheet to refer to as you read on and begin using the tool.

The test drive is organized into nine steps to familiarize you with the full range of the map's functional and structural elements. As you read the rest of this chapter, we recommend that you apply a learn–do approach: read about a feature and then try it. Enter fictional data for functions and steps, and include parallel (concurrent) activities for at least one step. Use the custom toolbar to insert, remove, and move steps and functions; define and undefine the timeline critical path; insert comments; perform a spell check; audit the map, and so on. Since you have created a test file to work with, you are safe to experiment. *But during both the test drive and regular mapping use, do not forget to save your work frequently.*

We will begin our test drive with the current-state MBPM. Since you have already opened the file, the Current State sheet should be active.

Step 1: Complete the Header

The map header houses general information related to the process being mapped and the team involved. Complete the cells as described here.

■ **PT Units and LT Units:** As shown in Figure 6.12, select the radio button for the unit of measure associated with the process and lead times for each step. The PT and LT units of measure are taken into account when the tool calculates the summary metrics, so it is critical that this button is marked correctly and it is critical that you use these same units of measure consistently while mapping. If you forget to select the units of measure, the audit tool will generate a corrective

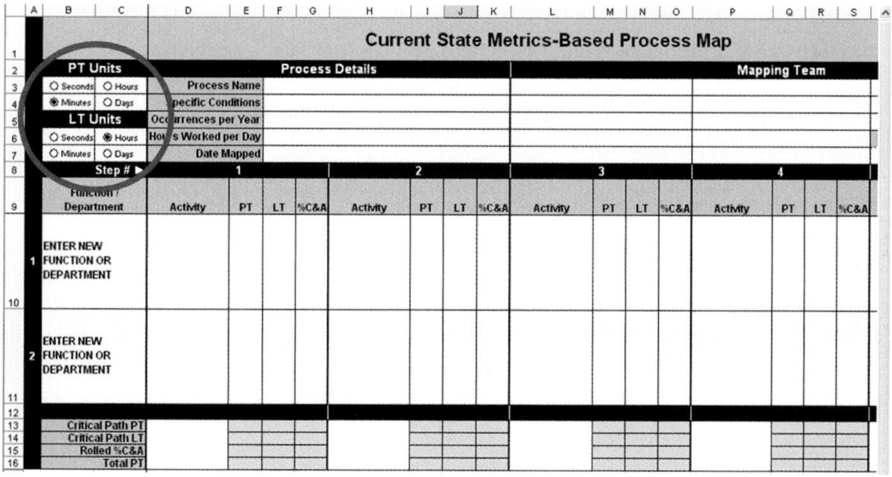

Figure 6.12   Process Time (PT) and Lead Time (LT) units of measure; radio button options.

action message that reminds you to select the appropriate units of measure. *Mapping tip:* The lead time is often expressed in one or more units of measure higher than the process time. Refer to Chapter 4 for more information about selecting units of measure. (*Note:* Changing the unit of measure radio button does not autoconvert the PT or LT values entered. If you change the units of measure while mapping, you must reenter the PT or LT values to correspond to the new unit of measure.)

■ **Process Details:** Complete the Process Details section as follows:

Process Name: Enter the name of the process being mapped. Use a name that is descriptive so that anyone viewing the file will clearly understand which process the map represents.

Specific Conditions: This cell houses the specific conditions or situations that are included or excluded in the map (if relevant). For example, you may have mapped the order entry process for first-time customers only. Or, you may have mapped a patient flow process for urgent care only—or the quoting process for a specific product line, in a specific part of the country, during a specific time of the year, and/or for a specific customer group. In the first example, the process name might be "order entry" and the specific conditions may be defined as "first-time customers."

Occurrences per Year: Here, you enter "customer demand"— the number of times the mapped process is performed per year. This value is used to calculate labor requirements, expressed as the number of full-time equivalent employees (FTEs) required to perform the process (discussed in Chapter 4).

Hours Worked per Day: This is the approximate number of clock hours the employees who support the process being mapped are scheduled to work per day. Many office, service, and technical environments work an average of 8 hours per day. But some of these environments run 2 or 3 shifts per day. In this case, list the total number of hours per day the operation is typically open for business. Therefore, if the staff works typical office hours, enter "8." If the process is performed by employees on two 8-hour shifts, enter "16." Enter "24" if the operation runs around the clock. If the scheduled work hours vary between departments represented on the map, select the number of hours worked by either the majority of the functions, or the hours worked by the function that is most critical to the process. The value you enter into the Hours Worked per Day cell is critical in converting hours to business days (and vice versa).

Date Mapped: Enter the date the map was manually created by the cross-functional team, not the date it was electronically documented in the MBPM tool. Dates convert to the international format (e.g., 16-Aug-12).

■ **Mapping Team:** Enter the first and last names of the individuals who participated in the manual mapping process, one name per cell. If the map was created during a Kaizen Event, enter the team member names here. Enter the name of the mapping facilitator in the cell below the facilitator label.

Step 2: Insert Functions and Steps

Before entering data for the process steps themselves, you must create the space for the activities and accompanying metrics. This is accomplished by inserting rows to house the functions, departments, work groups, and so forth, that are involved in the process (e.g., order entry, patient intake, product development, finance, shipping, sales, nursing, accounts payable, payroll, data entry, and so on), and columns that represent sequential steps in the process. The location and orientation of functions and steps are displayed in Figure 6.13. The master file comes preloaded with two functions and five steps, the minimum number the tool requires to function properly.

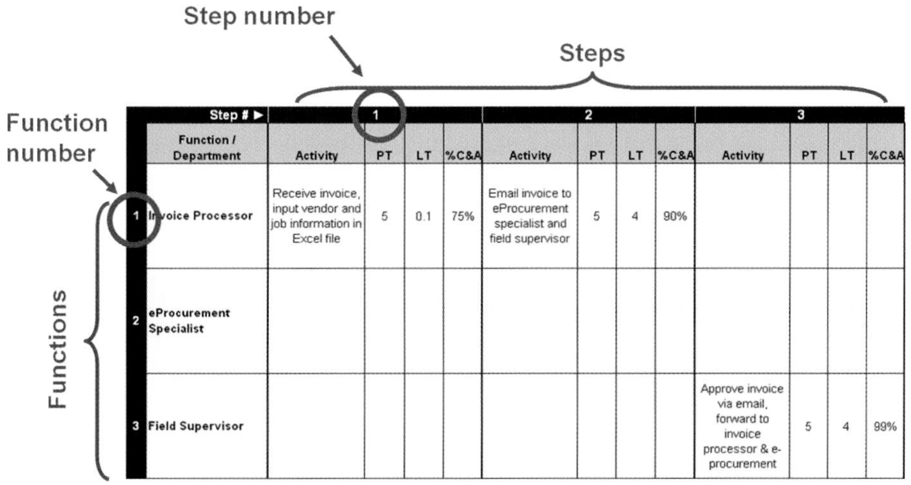

Figure 6.13   Orientation of functions and steps.

Functions and steps can be added or removed one by one or as a group. When you are initially setting up your map to prepare for data entry, it is easiest to insert them all at once as follows:

- **Insert functions:** Count the number of functions (swim lanes) represented on the manually created map. Click the **Insert** option on the custom toolbar and select **Insert Function(s)** from the drop-down menu. In the Insert Function(s) pop-up window (Figure 6.14), enter the number of functions you wish to add (remember that the map comes preloaded with two functions already), and indicate where, within the existing function numbers, you would like your new function(s) to be inserted. *Note:* If you insert a large number of functions, you may experience a short delay as the macro executes the command.

- **Insert steps:** Steps can also be added one by one or all at once as a group. As with functions, when you are initially setting up your map to prepare for data entry, it's easiest to insert steps all at once. First, count the number of steps (Post-its positioned in one vertical plane) represented on the manual map from which you are working. Then repeat the steps described in Step 1 above, using the **Insert Step(s)** option on the **Insert** drop-down menu. Remember that the map comes preloaded with five steps. *Note:* If you add new steps or activities within existing steps after you have defined the timeline critical path, you must redefine the timeline critical path, as described in Step 4 below.

- **Remove functions or steps:** If you wish to remove a single function or step, or a group of consecutive functions or steps, select the **Remove** option on the custom toolbar, and enter the desired range of consecutive functions or steps you wish to remove in the pop-up window. If you wish to remove only one function or step, enter its number in both boxes in the pop-up window. As a reminder, the tool is designed to include

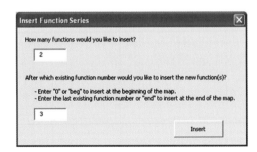

Figure 6.14   Insert function pop-up window.

a minimum of two functions and five steps on the current- and future-state maps. Therefore, you will not be permitted to remove steps and functions beyond those minimums. If the function(s) or step(s) you wish to remove contains data, you will receive a pop-up warning asking you to validate your intent. Type "Yes" if you want to proceed. This feature is designed to prevent the accidental removal of a function or step that contains activities.

If you wish to rearrange a function's placement, select **Move > Move Function** on the custom toolbar. In the resulting pop-up window, enter the function number you wish to move. A second pop-up window will appear, prompting you for the function's destination. Enter the function number where you would like the moved function to appear. All of the functions below the new one will shift down one position and will automatically renumber themselves. A similar option exists for steps, Move Step. When the step is moved to a new location, all steps affected by the move will automatically renumber.

Once you have grown comfortable with adding, removing, and moving functions and steps, enter at least two function names and data for at least five steps, and proceed to Step 3.

Step 3: Enter Data for Each Step

In this step and as shown in Figure 6.15, you will enter data into the activity, PT, LT, and %C&A cells in the body of the map you created in Step 2. You can choose to enter data into the map either one step at a time (including all parallel activities) or one function at a time. To avoid data entry errors and omissions, it is best to stick with a standard approach. One step at a time typically works best.

Activity

The activity descriptions should be written in a verb/noun format to highlight the action involved (e.g., "receive quote," "enter customer complaint," "verify credit," "audit report," and so forth) as shown in Figure 6.15. Create clear and concise descriptions. The activity cells are formatted to wrap text. If all of the data you have entered is not visible, you may take one of three actions: (1) shorten your description, (2) reduce the font size, or (3) insert a comment (using the **Insert/Modify Comment** feature on the custom toolbar) to house the overflow information. (*Note:* The viewing area of the comment box is limited to the first 95 or so characters of content, depending on the width of the letters involved.)

Step #	1			
Function/ Department	Activity	PT	LT	%
Invoice Processor	Receive invoice, input vendor and job information in Excel file	5	0.1	75%

Figure 6.15   Sample activity with metrics.

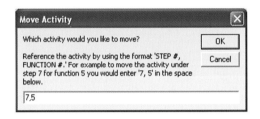

Figure 6.16   Move activity pop-up window.

If you need to move an activity to another position on the map, click the **Move** option on the custom toolbar and select the **Move Activity** option from the drop-down menu. In the resulting pop-up window (Figure 6.16), enter the step and function number separated by a comma for the activity you wish to move, followed by the step and function number for the location to which you wish to move the activity. The activity *and its associated metrics* will move to the desired location. *Note:* Do not enter the actual cell numbers as you would in a regular Excel workbook. Within the MBPM tool, step and function numbers are needed to execute insert, remove, and/or move commands.

If you attempt to move an activity and its metrics to a location that already contains an activity and metrics, a warning pop-up window will give you the option of overwriting the destination cells or canceling the Move Activity operation. You must type "Yes" in the space provided to overwrite, otherwise click **Cancel** or hit the Escape key to abort the move.

Note: If you have already defined the timeline critical path (explained further in Step 4) and move an activity, you will need to redefine the timeline critical path for all steps affected by the move.

Process Time (PT)

Enter the process time ("touch time") in the PT cells that correspond to each activity. Be sure the number you enter corresponds with the PT unit of measure you selected in Step 1 above. When you enter the first PT value for a particular step, the corresponding Total PT cell on the Step Summary section at the bottom of the map will autopopulate with that same value. If you enter PTs for two or more functions for a particular step, the Total PT cell progressively reflects the cumulative PT for that step. Total PT is a factor in calculating labor requirements (described in Step 7).

When you define the timeline critical path, the critical path step's PT will autopopulate the timeline critical path PT cell for that step. Once you have defined the timeline critical path, if you alter the PT for a step that contains parallel activities, the timeline critical path is automatically undefined and you will need to redefine it.

Lead Time (LT)

Enter the lead time (throughput time or turnaround time) in the LT cells that correspond to each activity. Be sure the numbers you enter correspond with the LT unit of measure you selected in Step 1. The same holds true for LT as with PT in regard to the timeline critical path.

Percent Complete and Accurate (%C&A)

Enter the percent complete and accurate in the %C&A cells that correspond to each activity, as determined by the downstream customers who receive output from the step in question. When you enter the first %C&A value for a particular step, the corresponding Rolled %C&A cell in the Step Summary section at the bottom of the map will autopopulate with that same value. If you enter %C&As for two or more functions for a particular step, the Rolled %C&A cell progressively reflects the product of *all* of the %C&A values for that step, which illustrates the multiplier effect that poor quality has on a process. Rolled %C&A values serve as source data for the cumulative Rolled %C&A metric on the Summary Metrics sheet (described in Step 7).

A special circumstance exists when assessing the output quality for a series of consecutive steps performed by the same individual. In most cases, only one of the consecutive steps produces the output that is evaluated for quality by downstream customers, and all of the other steps are assumed to be 100 percent quality. Please refer to Chapter 4 for further information on how to treat this circumstance.

An additional special circumstance exists when a customer, many steps downstream from a particular step, assesses the output quality from that step to be poorer than did the immediate customer. In this case, *multiply the %C&As reported by all downstream customers to calculate the %C&A for a particular supplier's output.*

Spell Check

If you would like to spell check your work, open the sheet you would like to check and select the **Spell Check Active Sheet** option from the **Map Management** drop-down list on the custom toolbar. This activates the spell check feature on the active sheet only. The spell check feature is only functional on the current-state and future-state sheets. *Note:* The spell check feature will not recognize MBPM-specific terms such as %C&A. When the spell checker highlights this acronym, you may select either **Ignore All** or **Add to Dictionary**. If you add it to your dictionary, you will never be asked again about this term, which can save time on future maps.

Notes and Visuals

Row eight is designed to accommodate user-defined content in order to further visualize or add explanatory material, for example, color coding or labeling specific segments of the process, categorizing each step as value-adding or non-value-adding, and so on.

Clearing the Map

If for any reason you want to delete *all* of the data you have entered in the current-state map (including the header information, function names, activities, and metrics), select **Clear Current State MBPM** from the **Map Management** section of the custom toolbar. As a precaution, you will be asked if you are sure you want to execute this action. Type "Yes" in the window if you are sure you want to clear the map of all contents. A similar option exists for clearing the content of future-state maps; select **Clear Future State MBPM**.

Step 4: Define the Timeline Critical Path

Once you have entered the activities and metrics for all current-state process steps, the timeline critical path must be defined. As explained in Chapter 4, a timeline critical path exists where activities occur in parallel; that is, work is being performed concurrently. The drop-down menu within the Map Management section of the custom toolbar includes three critical path-related options: Define Critical Path, Undefine Critical Path, and Add Activity to Critical Path.

When you are ready to define the timeline critical path for a newly created map, select **Define Critical Path** from the **Map Management** drop-down menu. As the macro reviews your map from Step 1 forward, the activity and metrics cells (PT, LT, and %C&A) for any step for which there are no parallel activities are automatically color-coded blue, indicating they are part of the timeline critical path, as shown in Figure 6.17.

When the macro reaches a step that contains parallel (concurrent) activities, it generates a pop-up window that displays all of the functions, activities, and associated lead times that occur within that step, and asks you to select which of those activities should be part of the timeline critical path. Enter the function number for the timeline critical path activity, which will color-code the cells containing the selected activity and its associated metrics blue.

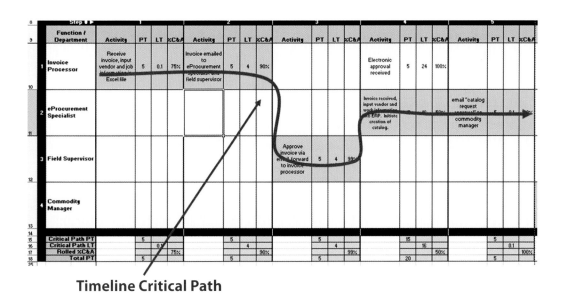

Timeline Critical Path

Figure 6.17   Timeline critical path.

As described more fully in Chapter 4, when you compare activities performed in parallel, the timeline critical path is typically comprised of the sequence of activities with the longest cumulative LT. An exception exists if the output from a parallel activity with the longest lead time constitutes a dead end; that is, the work does not ultimately reach the customer.

Note: Even if your map contains no parallel activities, the MBPM tool requires you to define a timeline critical path, because this action drives several of the summary metrics calculations. Also, as a mistake-proofing measure, if you make any modifications to the map after the timeline critical path has been defined, you must redefine the timeline critical path and audit (or reaudit) the map to generate the summary metrics. The audit feature is introduced in step 5.

To redefine the timeline critical path, click on the cell containing the activity you wish to add to the timeline critical path and select the **Add Activity to Critical Path** command from the **Map Management** section of the custom toolbar. The macro will update the relevant summary metrics, convert the highlighted step to blue, and remove the blue color-coding as previously determined. Alternatively, you may select the **Define Critical Path** option. The program will retain the timeline critical path for those steps that are already defined, automatically select new or moved activities that are not in parallel, and ask you to select the timeline critical path activity when it reaches a step for which the timeline critical path is not defined.

Once you have defined (or redefined) the timeline critical path, the Critical Path PT, and Critical Path LT cells in the Step Summary section at the bottom of the map will autopopulate (Figure 6.18).

If you want to reevaluate your map and redefine the timeline critical path, you may select the **Undefine Critical Path** option from the **Map Management** section of the custom toolbar. Executing this command will undefine the timeline critical path for the entire map. You may redefine the timeline critical path by following the previous steps.

Critical Path PT		5			5	
Critical Path LT			0.1			4
Rolled %C&A				75%			90%
Total PT		5			5	

Figure 6.18   Step Summary data.

Note: After you've defined the timeline critical path *and your map is in final form*, you may wish to differentiate the types of process activities by manually color-coding the activity cells. Excel's green, yellow, and red fill colors are a convenient way to depict value-adding, necessary non-value-adding, and unnecessary non-value-adding activities, respectively. If you define the timeline critical path after you've manually color-coded the activity cells, all timeline critical path activities will convert to blue. Also, if you undefine the timeline critical path, all cells revert to yellow. An additional feature resides in row 8, Notes & Visuals. These white cells above each step can be used for descriptions, comments, or color-coding for specific segments of a process. Many users have employed this cell to visualize phases of the process (e.g., quoting, ordering, and fulfillment). Text in row 8 is formatted to shrink to fit. If a step is moved or deleted, the content is handled similarly.

Step 5: Audit the Map

After you have completed the current-state map and the timeline critical path has been defined, you must audit your maps to assure they meet the requirements necessary to calculate the summary metrics. *The Summary Metrics sheet will not autopopulate until you audit your maps, resolve any audit findings that are generated, and receive a congratulations message indicating your map meets all audit requirements.* To audit your map, select the **Audit Current State MBPM** option on the **Map Management** drop-down menu. The Audit Findings sheet automatically opens and lists the corrective actions you must take (Figure 6.19). If your map meets all audit requirements, you will receive a congratulations message. When you click **OK** on the congratulations message, the tool will autonavigate to the Summary Metrics page.

If the Audit Findings sheet lists a number of corrective actions, you may want to print the sheet so you can resolve the issues without having to toggle back and forth between the Audit Findings sheet and the map. When you

MBPM Audit Findings	
Current State MBPM Findings	**Future State MBPM Findings**
1. PT units must be selected on the Current State Map.	1. Future State map has not been audited.
2. Hours Worked per Day must contain numerical data.	
3. Step 1, Function 2: missing data in at least one cell.	
4. Step 1: must be added to the critical path.	
5. Step 4, Function 1: missing data in at least one cell.	

Figure 6.19   Audit findings.

have taken the recommended corrective actions, audit the map again. Repeat the cycle until you receive the congratulations message indicating that your map meets all requirements. At the same time you receive the congratulations message, the corresponding metrics section of the Summary Metrics sheet autopopulates. A similar feature exists for the future-state map.

Remember: If you modify data in the activity, PT, LT, or %C&A cells after you have defined the timeline critical path, you will need to redefine the timeline critical path and reaudit in order for the summary metrics to autocalculate.

Step 6: Document the Future State

You can document the future-state map in one of two ways: (1) Once your current-state map meets all audit requirements, you may copy the current-state map by selecting the **Copy Current State MBPM to Future State MBPM** feature from the **Map Management** drop-down menu on the custom toolbar, and then modify the map to reflect the future state, or (2) Create the future-state map from scratch. Creating a future-state map from scratch may be easier when the future state is dramatically different from the current state (e.g., you have removed several functions and/or steps or the work will be heavily reallocated). If you choose this option, select the Future State sheet and repeat mapping Steps 1 through 5.

Copying the current-state map is best when it would be quicker and easier to rely on the current-state map as a foundation. If you choose this option, all of the contents of the current-state map will be copied to the future-state map, including the header information (PT and LT units, map details, and mapping team members), metrics, step summary totals, and the defined timeline critical path.

When you select the **Copy Current State MBPM to Future State MBPM** command, a pop-up window will ask you to confirm that you want to copy the current-state map and overwrite all future-state map contents. Type "Yes" in the window and click **OK**. The future-state sheet will open automatically and you can begin modifying the map to reflect your desired future state.

Review the header information on the future-state MBPM and make any appropriate modifications (e.g., PT or LT units of measure, projected number of occurrences, or date mapped). Use the Map Management tools as described in Steps 2 and 3 to insert and remove functions and steps, move activities, and modify the data to reflect the projected improved state. When your future-state map is complete, perform the spell check, then define the timeline critical path and audit the map as described in Steps 4 and 5 above.

If for any reason you want to delete *all* of the data you have entered in the future-state map (header information, function names, activities, and metrics), select **Clear Future State MBPM** from the **Map Management** section of the custom toolbar. A mistake-proofing warning will require you to enter "Yes" to execute the command.

Step 7: Review the Summary Metrics Sheet

When the current- and future-state maps meet all audit requirements (i.e., no further corrective actions are suggested on the Audit Findings sheet and you have received congratulations messages that both maps meet all requirements), the Predefined Performance Metrics and Capacity Calculations sections of the Summary Metrics sheet (Figure 6.20) will display summary

							0 Decimal Places
	Summary Metrics						1 Decimal Place
							2 Decimal Places
Predefined Performance Metrics							
	Current State		**Projected Future State**		**Desired Direction**		**Projected**
Metric	Value	Units	Value	Units	Up	Down	**Improvement**
Critical Path PT Sum	165.0	minutes	153.0	minutes		☟	7.3%
Critical Path LT Sum	10.0	hours	3.5	hours		☟	65.0%
Activity Ratio	27.5	%	72.9	%	☟		164.9%
Rolled % C&A	9.0	%	30.1	%	☟		233.4%
# of Activities	8	activities	5	activities		☟	37.5%
Capacity Calculations							
	Current State		**Projected Future State**				**Projected**
Metric	Value	Units	Value	Units			**Change**
Sum of Total PTs	160.0	minutes	148.0	minutes			-7.50%
Occurrences per Year	5000	occurrences	5000	occurrences			0.0%
Available Work Hours per Year	1800	hours	1800	hours			0.0%
Labor Requirements	7.4	FTEs	6.9	FTEs			-7.5%
User-defined Performance Metrics							
	Current State		**Projected Future State**		**Desired Direction**		**Projected**
Metric	Value	Units	Value	Units	Up	Down	**Improvement**
Number of Departments	4.0	Departments	2.0	Departments	☐	☟	50.0%
					☐	☐	
					☐	☐	
					☐	☐	
					☐	☐	
					☐	☐	
					☐	☐	
					☐	☐	
					☐	☐	
					☐	☐	

Figure 6.20   Summary metrics sheet.

data as well as projected improvement values. (*Note:* As a reminder, these metrics are defined on the Metrics Descriptions sheet.) You may select the desired number of decimal places by clicking the appropriate decimal button above the Projected Improvement column.

The Desired Direction columns drive the Projected Improvement column color-coding conventions as well as the hidden formulas that are used to calculate the results. Cells containing projected improvement percentages in which the future-state results are projected to move in the desired direction are color-coded green. If the change is projected to move in an undesired direction, the projected improvement values will carry negative signs and the cells will be color-coded orange. Cells are color-coded salmon/tan if no change is projected to occur.

The Summary Metrics sheet also includes space for up to ten user-defined performance metrics (yellow color-coded cells). These cells are provided if you want to track additional metrics, such as productivity, number of handoffs, equipment uptime, financial measures, number of software applications accessed, specific rework loops or quality measures, industry- and process-specific measurements, PT for a particular functional area, morale improvement, and so forth. Since these metrics are user-defined, you will need to manually populate these fields, including the current-state and future-state values, units of measure, and the desired direction of change (up or down).

Step 8: Print the Map

If you would like a hard copy of your map, the tool is designed to print landscape on 8.5 × 11-inch paper, with up to 5 steps and 6 functions per page. For maps with multiple pages, the full map header prints on the first page only, and the pages are paginated sequentially from left to right. Each page includes a footer, which includes the file name you have selected, page numbers, and copyright information. The map can also be printed much larger using a plotter-style printer. Setup for successful plotter printed maps varies according to the printer.

Step 9: Distribute the Map

Completed MBPMs may be distributed by hard copy or electronically. Before distributing the map electronically, you should *lock the custom toolbar* to restrict unlicensed viewers' ability to create new or edit existing MBPMs (which violates the End User License Agreement). To lock the custom toolbar, select **Map Management > Lock MBPM Custom Toolbar** and enter a password containing at least four numbers or letters in the pop-up window. Save the file in its locked state. The file can now be distributed electronically. Recipients of an MBPM file with the toolbar locked will have the ability to review and print the file, but will not be able to perform any of the commands contained within the custom toolbar. To unlock the toolbar, go to **Map Management > Unlock MBPM Custom Toolbar** and enter the password that you entered in the pop-up window.

Another way to prevent unlicensed users from editing or creating maps is to use a PDF writer application (e.g., Adobe Professional, PDF995 freeware, etc.) to convert the map from Excel to a PDF format prior to distribution.

Troubleshooting

The MBPM tool has been carefully developed and tested thoroughly. However, using Excel as a platform presents a few challenges and carries with it some unique attributes with which inexperienced users may be unfamiliar. This section contains information for troubleshooting the tool should the need arise.

The Tool Closes Out or the Custom Toolbar Will Not Function

There are two versions of the MBPM tool on the accompanying CD; one is for users of Excel 2003, the other is for users of Excel 2007 and Excel 2010. Using the wrong file, a Macintosh computer, or failing to enable macros (see later in this chapter) will result in a pop-up message stating that the user is not running a current enough version of Excel for the tool to function properly and the MBPM tool will close. Users who have disabled macros will not receive the pop-up message, but they will not be able to use the custom toolbar, a requirement for the MBPM tool to function effectively.

Adjusting the Macro Security Settings

As discussed in the first section in this chapter, the MBPM tool contains macros that must be enabled for the tool to function properly. Enabling

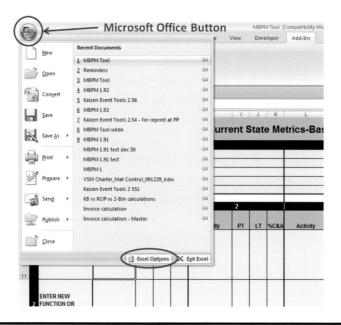

Figure 6.21 Adjusting macro security settings, Step 1.

macros may require you to adjust your macro security setting. We suggest setting macro security to Disable All Macros with Notification, but some users choose to set their security to Enable All Macros. To change the macro setting,* click the Microsoft Office button and select **Excel Options > Trust Center > Trust Center Settings > Macro Settings** (see Figures 6.21–6.23). If Disable All Macros with Notification is selected, a notification will appear in the Excel ribbon (Figure 6.2). To enable macros in this case, click **Options** and then select **Enable This Content**. If either Disable All Macros without Notification or Disable All Macros Except Digitally Signed Macros is selected (for Macro Settings options), macros will not be enabled and the MBPM tool will not function.

When you have modified the security setting, close and reopen the MBPM tool and enable the macros as described previously.

The Macros Will Not Execute

If an error message is received when you attempt to use one of the commands on the custom toolbar, you may not have enabled macros. To correct this, follow the directions given previously.

---

* See Appendix B for Excel 2003-specific instructions.

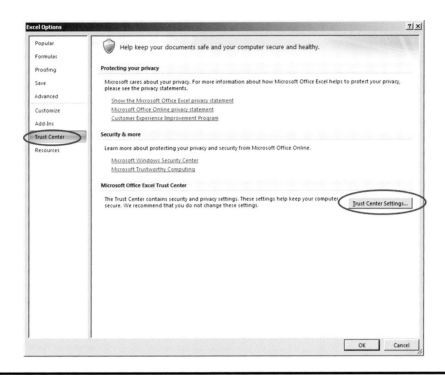

Figure 6.22   Adjusting macro security settings, Step 2.

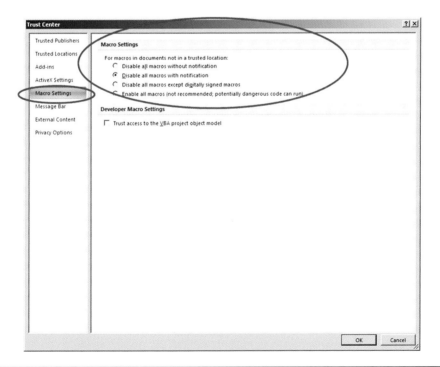

Figure 6.23   Adjusting macro security settings, Step 3.

The Cut, Copy, and Paste Commands Do Not Function

To ensure proper execution of the macros and formulas—and to preserve the tool's layout—Excel's cut, copy, and paste features have been disabled. Some of this functionality exists through the custom toolbar (e.g., Copy Current State MBPM to Future State MBPM, and the Remove, Insert, and Move commands).

The Undo Function Does Not Work

Excel's Undo command is not designed to undo actions executed through macros. Therefore, you will not be able to undo any actions you have taken using the custom toolbar features. Standard Undo functionality continues to operate for regular Excel actions.

Unable to Enter Information in a Cell

You may enter data into yellow color-coded cells only. All other cells are locked to prevent formatting errors that could impact the macros and formulas designed into the tool. Additional information about color-coding and cell formatting is contained in Table 6.2.

The Tool Will Not Accommodate the Entire Process[*]

The tool will accommodate most processes that you would choose to map at a micro level. The number of process steps and functions that can be documented on a single map is limited only by the number of columns and rows available in Excel. Excel 2007 and 2010 offer significantly high numbers of rows for the tool to accommodate the number of functions that would be engaged in most any process. The MBPM tool for Excel versions 2007 and 2010 will accommodate over 4,000 process steps.

The Custom Toolbar Disappears[*]

This can happen if you are working on more than one MBPM file at the same time and you close one of the files, which closes the toolbar on all open MBPM files. To avoid this, work on only one MBPM file at a time.

---

[*] See Appendix B for Excel 2003–specific instructions.

If you must work with more than one MBPM file open at a time, keep all of the files open until you have finished editing all of the files. To have the custom toolbar reappear, close all of the open MBPM files, and then reopen the file that you need to work on. The custom toolbar will appear.*

The Custom Toolbar Will Not Work

The commands within the custom toolbar do not function in four circumstances: 1) you have not enabled macros (see previous sections for more information), 2) you are using an older version of Excel (earlier than 2003), or 3) you are in the edit mode within a cell (cursor is blinking) 4) you are using a Mac. Also, you must be in the normal navigation mode for Excel-based commands to function.

The Summary Metrics Sheet Is Blank

You must audit the maps, resolve all audit findings, reaudit, and receive the congratulations messages *on both the current-state and future-state maps* before the Summary Metrics sheet will autopopulate with each map's summary data.

File Size Is Extremely Large

The normal file size for a blank MBPM is approximately 700 K to 900 K. If the file size expands disproportionately relative to the amount of data you have loaded, check to see what version of Excel you are using. Users of Excel 2007 and 2010 who use the Excel 2003 file by mistake may experience massive expansion in file size (40 MB or more). If you are using Excel 2007 or 2010, use the MBPM 2007 and 2010.xlsm file to avoid this problem.

Delay When Using Custom Toolbar Commands

Due to the increased number of rows and columns available in Excel 2007 and 2010, the user may experience a slight delay when using the Insert, Remove, and Copy Current State to Future State features on the Custom Toolbar.

---

* See Appendix B for Excel 2003–specific instructions.

Chapter 7

Process Management

Let's say you've committed to systematically improving one of your key processes, you've gone through an initial round of improvement, and you've both documented the new standard work and you've trained everyone involved on the new way of operating. Now what? What you *don't* want to do is move on to the next problem to be solved or the next process to be improved and never look back. Sustaining improvement is where the rubber meets the road and many hours of well-intended effort can go down the drain.

The Plan-Do-Study-Adjust (PDSA) cycle isn't linear for good reason. Once an initial round of improvement is complete, you'll need to continuously study how the process is performing and take corrective action (via another PDSA cycle) if and when performance begins to trend away from your target metrics. Even if the process consistently performs as designed, this news is no reason to rest on one's laurels. Consistently good performance becomes the new *business as usual* and indicates that it's time to go through another round of improvement to set the bar higher. This is the essence of continuous improvement.

Who determines whether corrective action is needed and drives ongoing improvement? A process owner. We don't mean an owner at the strategic level, such as a vice president or director. We mean a tactical owner who's responsible for the overall performance of the process, and ongoing improvement of the process *across all the functions it touches*. This person keeps an eagle eye on the daily performance of the process, identifying out-of-standard conditions and surfacing opportunities for improvement.

In most organizations, the process owner concept has yet to be embraced, which is the single biggest obstacle to sustaining improvements. It is inappropriate to place individuals who are not very close to the process in the role of process owner, so don't expect people from the continuous improvement department to have the focus, time, or understanding to effectively drive day-to-day process management or improvement. Similarly, leaders who are too far removed from day-to-day activities to "mind the store" will not have the insights or bandwidth to do the role justice.

You will need to help your organization break its habit of assuming processes will simply work as designed, that people will perform as they were trained, and that siloed management will optimize overall process performance. The natural state of all systems is entropy (chaos). It takes concerted effort to avert entropy, and even greater effort to regain control of your processes if and when entropy ensues. In our experience, clear and disciplined process ownership is the first step to sustaining improvements as designed and baking continuous improvement into your organization's DNA.

The second must-do for sustaining improvement is implementing visual management to track process performance. Ideally, you've implemented some sort of visual management through the course of making improvements. But if you haven't, this is the time to do so. Process performance is best tracked via leading indicators, which often include metrics related to customer service, quality of work, and cost or effectiveness. Without creating a highly visual means to track real-time performance against your targets, the need for problem solving and improvement will remain hidden.

As with making improvement, designing the way you'll shine a light on process performance needs to be a cross-functional activity involving the people who actually do the work. It should not be a manager or senior leader's sole decision. Once work teams grow comfortable with having relevant metrics visually displayed and properly managed (slipping performance stimulates the need for additional improvement, not reprimands), they won't want to go back to the old days when managers and process workers knew neither how processes were truly performing—nor how they *should*.

Process management is as much an art as science. And we recognize that continuously improving every key process is a tall order in organizations that are just beginning to look at their processes in systematic fashion we promote in this book. But to achieve any level of operational excellence, organizations have to begin working on the business as much as they work *in* the business. It's the only way to transform from a fire-fighting culture to a fire-prevention culture.

How should you begin? Clearly define the problem you wish to solve. Carefully scope the process (or one of the processes) involved, form a relevant cross-functional team, gain a deep understanding about the current state (often through the creation of a current-state metrics-based process map), perform root-cause analysis as needed, design the future state, execute, and begin managing the new process. These steps comprise the Plan and Do phases of a high-level Plan-Do-Study-Adjust (PDSA) cycle. And then reflect. Study how the process for improving worked for the organization and what may need to be adjusted for the next process you tackle. While you're continuing to monitor performance resulting from the initial round of improvement (and taking corrective action and continuously improving as necessary—the Study and Adjust phases), select the next process for study and improvement. And repeat. With time, process owners will be in place for all of your key processes, providing the management and continuous improvement that each of those processes warrants, and you will have transformed yourself into a continuous improvement culture.

With each successive round of improvement, you'll notice a reduction in the level of internal chaos you've had to contend with. You'll notice higher levels of customer and employee satisfaction. You'll notice that costs are falling off your general ledger without being fully aware where exactly the reductions are coming from. As the chief executive officer (CEO) for one of our clients has said:

> "In my experience leading organizations through the Lean journey, there's a magic moment, a tipping point, where a critical mass of believers engage their hearts and souls into making their work simpler and easier. All of the organization training, kaizen events, action teams, finally kick into a natural unconscious behavior. The power of incremental improvements creates inertia that delivers profit to the bottom line. No one is really sure what exactly is driving the financial improvements. It's not an event; it's a change of culture: a new healthier, happier company. That's what I call the magic of Lean."

Metrics-Based Process Mapping provides the disciplined approach and methodology you need to identify and reduce waste and to drive continuous improvement. We hope this book has provided you with the step-by-step approach you need to be successful and play a pivotal role in your organization's transformation. Because there's nothing more satisfying in the world of problem solving and business management than making improvement and seeing it last. Let us know how it goes.

Appendix A: Excel Tool Quick Start Guide

While the Metrics-Based Process Mapping (MBPM) Excel tool is designed to be intuitive, most users will benefit from reading Chapter 6 before using the tool. However, experienced Excel users may be able to begin using the tool after reading this Quick Start Guide.

Note: 1) This tool was created for PCs operating with Excel 2003 or later. It does not function on earlier versions of Excel or on Mac operating systems. 2) This tool is intended for use only after maps have been manually created in a team-based environment.

Excel Tool Overview

As shown in Figure A.1, the tool contains a custom toolbar (accessible via the Add-Ins pull-down menu in Excel 2007 and 2010) and 10 sheets, accessed by tabs at the bottom of the Excel workspace. The four toolbar features— Insert, Remove, Move, and Map Management—produce drop-down menus of actions that simplify the mapping process. The functions/departments involved in the process are structured as rows and the steps in the process appear as columns.

Each step contains one or more activities and its three key metrics for each: process time (PT), lead time (LT), and percent complete and accurate (%C&A). The cells on the MBPM tool are color-coded according to function:

- **Yellow:** Accepts user data entry.
- **Salmon/tan:** Autopopulated with data from other cells or the results from programmed formulas.
- **Blue:** Timeline critical path activities.

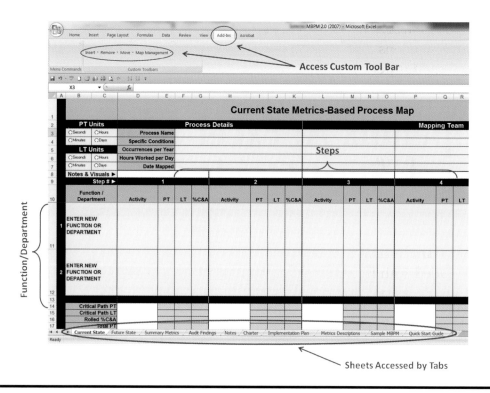

Figure A.1   Tool overview.

To Begin

Open the appropriate MBPM worksheet (Excel 2003* or Excel 2007 and 2010), enable macros, and agree to the End User License Agreement. Save the file with a unique name in the desired folder. Document the manually-produced map as follows.

Step 1: Complete the Header

- **PT Units & LT Units:** Select the unit of measure that will be used when entering the process times and lead times for each process step.
- **Process Name:** Enter the name of the process being documented.
- **Specific Conditions:** Enter any specific conditions (e.g., "first time customers only" or "domestic sales") pertaining to the process being mapped.
- **Occurrences per Year:** Enter how many times the process is performed each year (customer demand).

---

* See Appendix B for Excel 2003–specific instructions.

- **Hours Worked per Day:** Enter how many clock hours per day the functions that perform the process are scheduled to work.
- **Date Mapped:** Enter the date the process was manually mapped.
- **Mapping Team:** Enter the names of the individuals who participated when the process was manually mapped.

Step 2: Add Functions and Steps

Count the number of functions (horizontal swim lanes) and columns of steps (Post-its®) on the manually produced map. Add rows for the functions and columns for steps by selecting the **Insert** feature on the custom toolbar and **Insert Function(s)** or **Insert Step(s)** from the drop-down menu. The tool is preloaded with five steps and two functions, the minimum number of steps and functions required for the tool to operate.

Step 3: Enter Data for Each Step

Enter process activities (tasks) using a verb/noun format, and the associated PT, LT, and %C&A metrics for each. Be sure the units of measure for the values entered into the PT and LT cells match the units of measure selected in the header.

Step 4: Define the Timeline Critical Path

On the custom toolbar, select **Map Management Tools > Define Critical Path** to select which of the parallel (concurrent) activities comprise the timeline critical path. This step is required for the summary metrics to calculate correctly, even if the process being mapped has no parallel activities. When prompted, select the appropriate function (typically the one on the path with the longest lead time, as long as that activity does not lead to a dead end in the process). Timeline critical path activities will be color-coded blue. The white cells in row 8 above the step may be used for descriptive text or color-coding segments of the process if desired.

Step 5: Audit the Map

Select **Map Management > Audit Current State MBPM** on the custom toolbar. Correct the audit findings as needed and continue to reaudit until you receive a congratulations message. The Summary Metrics sheet will not autopopulate with relevant data until all audit findings are resolved.

Step 6: Document the Future State

Document the future-state map by either starting from scratch on the Future State tab or by copying the Current State sheet to the Future State sheet and modifying it accordingly. For the latter option, select **Map Management > Copy Current State MBPM to Future State MBPM** on the custom toolbar, and repeat Steps 1–5 above for the future-state map.

Step 7: Review the Summary Metrics Sheet

This sheet contains several predefined metrics. Enter additional user-defined metrics you want to track in the lower section.

Step 8: Print the Map (If Desired)

The tool is designed to be printed on 8.5 × 11-inch paper, with up to 5 steps and up to 5 functions per page. It can also be printed on large format plotter paper if desired.

Step 9: Distribute the Map

Prior to distributing the map to unlicensed users, lock the custom toolbar by selecting **Lock MBPM Custom Toolbar** from the **Map Management** drop-down menu. Licensed users may unlock the custom toolbar through the Map Management tool prior to editing the MBPM. You may also use a PDF writer to convert the map to PDF before distributing.

Additional Information

Additional information about metric-based process mapping and the MBPM tool is also available at: www.mbpmapping.com. Or you may contact Karen at www.ksmartin.com or Mike at www.mosterling.com.

Appendix B: Excel 2003–Specific Instructions

Enabling Macros

If your security level is set to medium (which is typically recommended for users who access Excel files containing macros on a regular basis), you will receive a message that requires you to select the Enable Macros option to ensure full functionality.

If your security level is set to very high or high, macros are automatically disabled. When you open the Metrics-Based Process Mapping (MBPM) file, you will receive a pop-up window that signals the need to adjust your security level to medium. From the Excel toolbar, select **Tools > Options > Security > Macro Security > Medium**, close the MBPM file, and reopen it. You will then receive the pop-up that allows you to enable macros and the tool will function properly.

If you do not enable macros for the MBPM tool, the custom toolbar will remain in your toolbar area, even after you have closed the MBPM tool. If this happens, you may remove the MBPM toolbar in one of two ways: 1) access Excel's standard toolbar features by choosing **View > Toolbars > Customize > Toolbars > MBPM > Delete**, or 2) reopen the MBPM file, enable macros, and close the file.

Custom Toolbar

Each time you open an MBPM file, a macro executes a command that adds a custom toolbar above the spreadsheet workspace. The exact location of the toolbar will vary depending on the number and size of the active toolbars on your computer. You may move the custom toolbar by placing your mouse over the vertical dots on the left side of the toolbar and dragging it to the desired location.

Adjusting the Macro Security Settings

If macro security is set to high or very high, you must adjust it to medium or lower (*Note:* setting it to low is not recommended), and then enable the macros when you open the MBPM tool. To set the security level to medium, select **Tools > Options > Security**. Click **Macro Security** and, in the resulting Security pop-up window, select **Medium** and **OK**. When you have modified the security setting, close and reopen the MBPM tool and enable the macros as described above.

The Tool Will Not Accommodate the Entire Process

Excel 2003 only contains 253 columns, so it limits the number of steps you can include in a single map to 63. If you are running Excel 2003 and your process has more than 63 linear steps (excludes parallel activities), you may either rescope the process to narrow your fence posts (first and last steps), or segment the process and create multiple maps. Excel 2007 and 2010 will accommodate over 4,000 process steps.

The Custom Toolbar Disappears

In Excel 2003, the custom toolbar may disappear if you mistakenly unclick the MBPM option in View > Toolbars. To have it appear again, simply click **MBPM** on the toolbar listing and it will reappear.

Index

About the Authors

Karen Martin has been building, managing, and improving operations for more than 20 years. As principal consultant for Karen Martin & Associates, LLC, she is a recognized thought leader in applying Lean thinking and the psychology of change to office, service, and knowledge work environments. Karen and her team provide transformation support to Fortune 100 companies, as well as small businesses, government agencies, nonprofits, and start-ups in diverse industries, such as construction, energy, financial services, government, healthcare, and manufacturing.

She is the author of *The Outstanding Organization* (McGraw-Hill, 2012) and coauthor of *The Kaizen Event Planner* (CRC Press, 2007) an instructor for the University of California, San Diego's Lean Enterprise program, and an industry advisor to the University of San Diego's Industrial and Systems Engineering program. For more information, visit www.ksmartin.com.

Mike Osterling provides support and leadership to manufacturing and non-manufacturing organizations on their Lean Transformation Journey. In a continuous improvement leadership role for six years, Mike played a key role in Square D Company's Lean transformation in the 1990s. His clients include small and large companies in manufacturing, construction, energy, and medical, as well as public agencies.

Mike led the development of the Lean Enterprise Certificate Program at San Diego State University and has taught in the program since 1999. He is also an instructor at the University of California, San Diego, is a Certified Trainer for the Implementation of Lean Manufacturing, a Six Sigma Black Belt, and is fluent in Spanish. He also coauthored *The Kaizen Event Planner* (CRC Press, 2007). For more information, visit www.mosterling.com.